Mometrix

TEST PREPARATION

I0892284

Common Core Grade 7 English Language Arts Secrets Study Guide

DEAR FUTURE EXAM SUCCESS STORY

First of all, **THANK YOU** for purchasing Mometrix study materials!

Second, congratulations! You are one of the few determined test-takers who are committed to doing whatever it takes to excel on your exam. **You have come to the right place.** We developed these study materials with one goal in mind: to deliver you the information you need in a format that's concise and easy to use.

In addition to optimizing your guide for the content of the test, we've outlined our recommended steps for breaking down the preparation process into small, attainable goals so you can make sure you stay on track.

We've also analyzed the entire test-taking process, identifying the most common pitfalls and showing how you can overcome them and be ready for any curveball the test throws you.

Standardized testing is one of the biggest obstacles on your road to success, which only increases the importance of doing well in the high-pressure, high-stakes environment of test day. Your results on this test could have a significant impact on your future, and this guide provides the information and practical advice to help you achieve your full potential on test day.

Your success is our success

We would love to hear from you! If you would like to share the story of your exam success or if you have any questions or comments in regard to our products, please contact us at **800-673-8175** or **support@mometrix.com**.

Thanks again for your business and we wish you continued success!

Sincerely,
The Mometrix Test Preparation Team

Need more help? Check out our flashcards at:
http://MometrixFlashcards.com/CCSS

Written and edited by the Mometrix Exam Secrets Test Prep Team
Printed in the United States of America

TABLE OF CONTENTS

Introduction

Thank you for purchasing this resource! You have made the choice to prepare yourself for a test that could have a huge impact on your future, and this guide is designed to help you be fully ready for test day. Obviously, it's important to have a solid understanding of the test material, but you also need to be prepared for the unique environment and stressors of the test, so that you can perform to the best of your abilities.

For this purpose, the first section that appears in this guide is the **Secret Keys**. We've devoted countless hours to meticulously researching what works and what doesn't, and we've boiled down our findings to the five most impactful steps you can take to improve your performance on the test. We start at the beginning with study planning and move through the preparation process, all the way to the testing strategies that will help you get the most out of what you know when you're finally sitting in front of the test.

We recommend that you start preparing for your test as far in advance as possible. However, if you've bought this guide as a last-minute study resource and only have a few days before your test, we recommend that you skip over the first two Secret Keys since they address a long-term study plan.

If you struggle with **test anxiety**, we strongly encourage you to check out our recommendations for how you can overcome it. Test anxiety is a formidable foe, but it can be beaten, and we want to make sure you have the tools you need to defeat it.

Secret Key #1 – Plan Big, Study Small

There's a lot riding on your performance. If you want to ace this test, you're going to need to keep your skills sharp and the material fresh in your mind. You need a plan that lets you review everything you need to know while still fitting in your schedule. We'll break this strategy down into three categories.

Information Organization

Start with the information you already have: the official test outline. From this, you can make a complete list of all the concepts you need to cover before the test. Organize these concepts into groups that can be studied together, and create a list of any related vocabulary you need to learn so you can brush up on any difficult terms. You'll want to keep this vocabulary list handy once you actually start studying since you may need to add to it along the way.

Time Management

Once you have your set of study concepts, decide how to spread them out over the time you have left before the test. Break your study plan into small, clear goals so you have a manageable task for each day and know exactly what you're doing. Then just focus on one small step at a time. When you manage your time this way, you don't need to spend hours at a time studying. Studying a small block of content for a short period each day helps you retain information better and avoid stressing over how much you have left to do. You can relax knowing that you have a plan to cover everything in time. In order for this strategy to be effective though, you have to start studying early and stick to your schedule. Avoid the exhaustion and futility that comes from last-minute cramming!

Study Environment

The environment you study in has a big impact on your learning. Studying in a coffee shop, while probably more enjoyable, is not likely to be as fruitful as studying in a quiet room. It's important to keep distractions to a minimum. You're only planning to study for a short block of time, so make the most of it. Don't pause to check your phone or get up to find a snack. It's also important to **avoid multitasking**. Research has consistently shown that multitasking will make your studying dramatically less effective. Your study area should also be comfortable and well-lit so you don't have the distraction of straining your eyes or sitting on an uncomfortable chair.

The time of day you study is also important. You want to be rested and alert. Don't wait until just before bedtime. Study when you'll be most likely to comprehend and remember. Even better, if you know what time of day your test will be, set that time aside for study. That way your brain will be used to working on that subject at that specific time and you'll have a better chance of recalling information.

Finally, it can be helpful to team up with others who are studying for the same test. Your actual studying should be done in as isolated an environment as possible, but the work of organizing the information and setting up the study plan can be divided up. In between study sessions, you can discuss with your teammates the concepts that you're all studying and quiz each other on the details. Just be sure that your teammates are as serious about the test as you are. If you find that your study time is being replaced with social time, you might need to find a new team.

Secret Key #2 – Make Your Studying Count

You're devoting a lot of time and effort to preparing for this test, so you want to be absolutely certain it will pay off. This means doing more than just reading the content and hoping you can remember it on test day. It's important to make every minute of study count. There are two main areas you can focus on to make your studying count.

Retention

It doesn't matter how much time you study if you can't remember the material. You need to make sure you are retaining the concepts. To check your retention of the information you're learning, try recalling it at later times with minimal prompting. Try carrying around flashcards and glance at one or two from time to time or ask a friend who's also studying for the test to quiz you.

To enhance your retention, look for ways to put the information into practice so that you can apply it rather than simply recalling it. If you're using the information in practical ways, it will be much easier to remember. Similarly, it helps to solidify a concept in your mind if you're not only reading it to yourself but also explaining it to someone else. Ask a friend to let you teach them about a concept you're a little shaky on (or speak aloud to an imaginary audience if necessary). As you try to summarize, define, give examples, and answer your friend's questions, you'll understand the concepts better and they will stay with you longer. Finally, step back for a big picture view and ask yourself how each piece of information fits with the whole subject. When you link the different concepts together and see them working together as a whole, it's easier to remember the individual components.

Finally, practice showing your work on any multi-step problems, even if you're just studying. Writing out each step you take to solve a problem will help solidify the process in your mind, and you'll be more likely to remember it during the test.

Modality

Modality simply refers to the means or method by which you study. Choosing a study modality that fits your own individual learning style is crucial. No two people learn best in exactly the same way, so it's important to know your strengths and use them to your advantage.

For example, if you learn best by visualization, focus on visualizing a concept in your mind and draw an image or a diagram. Try color-coding your notes, illustrating them, or creating symbols that will trigger your mind to recall a learned concept. If you learn best by hearing or discussing information, find a study partner who learns the same way or read aloud to yourself. Think about how to put the information in your own words. Imagine that you are giving a lecture on the topic and record yourself so you can listen to it later.

For any learning style, flashcards can be helpful. Organize the information so you can take advantage of spare moments to review. Underline key words or phrases. Use different colors for different categories. Mnemonic devices (such as creating a short list in which every item starts with the same letter) can also help with retention. Find what works best for you and use it to store the information in your mind most effectively and easily.

Secret Key #3 – Practice the Right Way

Your success on test day depends not only on how many hours you put into preparing, but also on whether you prepared the right way. It's good to check along the way to see if your studying is paying off. One of the most effective ways to do this is by taking practice tests to evaluate your progress. Practice tests are useful because they show exactly where you need to improve. Every time you take a practice test, pay special attention to these three groups of questions:

- The questions you got wrong
- The questions you had to guess on, even if you guessed right
- The questions you found difficult or slow to work through

This will show you exactly what your weak areas are, and where you need to devote more study time. Ask yourself why each of these questions gave you trouble. Was it because you didn't understand the material? Was it because you didn't remember the vocabulary? Do you need more repetitions on this type of question to build speed and confidence? Dig into those questions and figure out how you can strengthen your weak areas as you go back to review the material.

Additionally, many practice tests have a section explaining the answer choices. It can be tempting to read the explanation and think that you now have a good understanding of the concept. However, an explanation likely only covers part of the question's broader context. Even if the explanation makes perfect sense, **go back and investigate** every concept related to the question until you're positive you have a thorough understanding.

As you go along, keep in mind that the practice test is just that: practice. Memorizing these questions and answers will not be very helpful on the actual test because it is unlikely to have any of the same exact questions. If you only know the right answers to the sample questions, you won't be prepared for the real thing. **Study the concepts** until you understand them fully, and then you'll be able to answer any question that shows up on the test.

It's important to wait on the practice tests until you're ready. If you take a test on your first day of study, you may be overwhelmed by the amount of material covered and how much you need to learn. Work up to it gradually.

On test day, you'll need to be prepared for answering questions, managing your time, and using the test-taking strategies you've learned. It's a lot to balance, like a mental marathon that will have a big impact on your future. Like training for a marathon, you'll need to start slowly and work your way up. When test day arrives, you'll be ready.

Start with the strategies you've read in the first two Secret Keys—plan your course and study in the way that works best for you. If you have time, consider using multiple study resources to get different approaches to the same concepts. It can be helpful to see difficult concepts from more than one angle. Then find a good source for practice tests. Many times, the test website will suggest potential study resources or provide sample tests.

Practice Test Strategy

If you're able to find at least three practice tests, we recommend this strategy:

Untimed and Open-Book Practice

Take the first test with no time constraints and with your notes and study guide handy. Take your time and focus on applying the strategies you've learned.

Timed and Open-Book Practice

Take the second practice test open-book as well, but set a timer and practice pacing yourself to finish in time.

Timed and Closed-Book Practice

Take any other practice tests as if it were test day. Set a timer and put away your study materials. Sit at a table or desk in a quiet room, imagine yourself at the testing center, and answer questions as quickly and accurately as possible.

Keep repeating timed and closed-book tests on a regular basis until you run out of practice tests or it's time for the actual test. Your mind will be ready for the schedule and stress of test day, and you'll be able to focus on recalling the material you've learned.

Secret Key #4 – Pace Yourself

Once you're fully prepared for the material on the test, your biggest challenge on test day will be managing your time. Just knowing that the clock is ticking can make you panic even if you have plenty of time left. Work on pacing yourself so you can build confidence against the time constraints of the exam. Pacing is a difficult skill to master, especially in a high-pressure environment, so **practice is vital**.

Set time expectations for your pace based on how much time is available. For example, if a section has 60 questions and the time limit is 30 minutes, you know you have to average 30 seconds or less per question in order to answer them all. Although 30 seconds is the hard limit, set 25 seconds per question as your goal, so you reserve extra time to spend on harder questions. When you budget extra time for the harder questions, you no longer have any reason to stress when those questions take longer to answer.

Don't let this time expectation distract you from working through the test at a calm, steady pace, but keep it in mind so you don't spend too much time on any one question. Recognize that taking extra time on one question you don't understand may keep you from answering two that you do understand later in the test. If your time limit for a question is up and you're still not sure of the answer, mark it and move on, and come back to it later if the time and the test format allow. If the testing format doesn't allow you to return to earlier questions, just make an educated guess; then put it out of your mind and move on.

On the easier questions, be careful not to rush. It may seem wise to hurry through them so you have more time for the challenging ones, but it's not worth missing one if you know the concept and just didn't take the time to read the question fully. Work efficiently but make sure you understand the question and have looked at all of the answer choices, since more than one may seem right at first.

Even if you're paying attention to the time, you may find yourself a little behind at some point. You should speed up to get back on track, but do so wisely. Don't panic; just take a few seconds less on each question until you're caught up. Don't guess without thinking, but do look through the answer choices and eliminate any you know are wrong. If you can get down to two choices, it is often worthwhile to guess from those. Once you've chosen an answer, move on and don't dwell on any that you skipped or had to hurry through. If a question was taking too long, chances are it was one of the harder ones, so you weren't as likely to get it right anyway.

On the other hand, if you find yourself getting ahead of schedule, it may be beneficial to slow down a little. The more quickly you work, the more likely you are to make a careless mistake that will affect your score. You've budgeted time for each question, so don't be afraid to spend that time. Practice an efficient but careful pace to get the most out of the time you have.

Secret Key #5 – Have a Plan for Guessing

When you're taking the test, you may find yourself stuck on a question. Some of the answer choices seem better than others, but you don't see the one answer choice that is obviously correct. What do you do?

The scenario described above is very common, yet most test takers have not effectively prepared for it. Developing and practicing a plan for guessing may be one of the single most effective uses of your time as you get ready for the exam.

In developing your plan for guessing, there are three questions to address:

- When should you start the guessing process?
- How should you narrow down the choices?
- Which answer should you choose?

When to Start the Guessing Process

Unless your plan for guessing is to select C every time (which, despite its merits, is not what we recommend), you need to leave yourself enough time to apply your answer elimination strategies. Since you have a limited amount of time for each question, that means that if you're going to give yourself the best shot at guessing correctly, you have to decide quickly whether or not you will guess.

Of course, the best-case scenario is that you don't have to guess at all, so first, see if you can answer the question based on your knowledge of the subject and basic reasoning skills. Focus on the key words in the question and try to jog your memory of related topics. Give yourself a chance to bring the knowledge to mind, but once you realize that you don't have (or you can't access) the knowledge you need to answer the question, it's time to start the guessing process.

It's almost always better to start the guessing process too early than too late. It only takes a few seconds to remember something and answer the question from knowledge. Carefully eliminating wrong answer choices takes longer. Plus, going through the process of eliminating answer choices can actually help jog your memory.

Summary: Start the guessing process as soon as you decide that you can't answer the question based on your knowledge.

How to Narrow Down the Choices

The next chapter in this book (**Test-Taking Strategies**) includes a wide range of strategies for how to approach questions and how to look for answer choices to eliminate. You will definitely want to read those carefully, practice them, and figure out which ones work best for you. Here though, we're going to address a mindset rather than a particular strategy.

Your odds of guessing an answer correctly depend on how many options you are choosing from.

Number of options left	5	4	3	2	1
Odds of guessing correctly	20%	25%	33%	50%	100%

You can see from this chart just how valuable it is to be able to eliminate incorrect answers and make an educated guess, but there are two things that many test takers do that cause them to miss out on the benefits of guessing:

- Accidentally eliminating the correct answer
- Selecting an answer based on an impression

We'll look at the first one here, and the second one in the next section.

To avoid accidentally eliminating the correct answer, we recommend a thought exercise called **the $5 challenge**. In this challenge, you only eliminate an answer choice from contention if you are willing to bet $5 on it being wrong. Why $5? Five dollars is a small but not insignificant amount of money. It's an amount you could afford to lose but wouldn't want to throw away. And while losing $5 once might not hurt too much, doing it twenty times will set you back $100. In the same way, each small decision you make—eliminating a choice here, guessing on a question there—won't by itself impact your score very much, but when you put them all together, they can make a big difference. By holding each answer choice elimination decision to a higher standard, you can reduce the risk of accidentally eliminating the correct answer.

The $5 challenge can also be applied in a positive sense: If you are willing to bet $5 that an answer choice *is* correct, go ahead and mark it as correct.

Summary: Only eliminate an answer choice if you are willing to bet $5 that it is wrong.

Which Answer to Choose

You're taking the test. You've run into a hard question and decided you'll have to guess. You've eliminated all the answer choices you're willing to bet $5 on. Now you have to pick an answer. Why do we even need to talk about this? Why can't you just pick whichever one you feel like when the time comes?

The answer to these questions is that if you don't come into the test with a plan, you'll rely on your impression to select an answer choice, and if you do that, you risk falling into a trap. The test writers know that everyone who takes their test will be guessing on some of the questions, so they intentionally write wrong answer choices to seem plausible. You still have to pick an answer though, and if the wrong answer choices are designed to look right, how can you ever be sure that you're not falling for their trap? The best solution we've found to this dilemma is to take the decision out of your hands entirely. Here is the process we recommend:

Once you've eliminated any choices that you are confident (willing to bet $5) are wrong, select the first remaining choice as your answer.

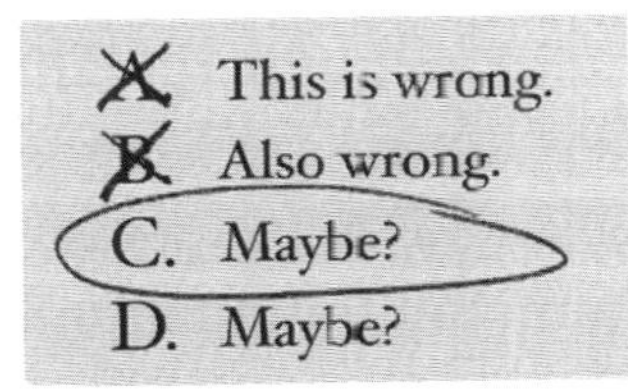

Whether you choose to select the first remaining choice, the second, or the last, the important thing is that you use some preselected standard. Using this approach guarantees that you will not be enticed into selecting an answer choice that looks right, because you are not basing your decision on how the answer choices look

This is not meant to make you question your knowledge. Instead, it is to help you recognize the difference between your knowledge and your impressions. There's a huge difference between thinking an answer is right because of what you know, and thinking an answer is right because it looks or sounds like it should be right.

Summary: To ensure that your selection is appropriately random, make a predetermined selection from among all answer choices you have not eliminated.

Test-Taking Strategies

This section contains a list of test-taking strategies that you may find helpful as you work through the test. By taking what you know and applying logical thought, you can maximize your chances of answering any question correctly!

It is very important to realize that every question is different and every person is different: no single strategy will work on every question, and no single strategy will work for every person. That's why we've included all of them here, so you can try them out and determine which ones work best for different types of questions and which ones work best for you.

Question Strategies

✓ Read Carefully

Read the question and the answer choices carefully. Don't miss the question because you misread the terms. You have plenty of time to read each question thoroughly and make sure you understand what is being asked. Yet a happy medium must be attained, so don't waste too much time. You must read carefully and efficiently.

✓ Contextual Clues

Look for contextual clues. If the question includes a word you are not familiar with, look at the immediate context for some indication of what the word might mean. Contextual clues can often give you all the information you need to decipher the meaning of an unfamiliar word. Even if you can't determine the meaning, you may be able to narrow down the possibilities enough to make a solid guess at the answer to the question.

✓ Prefixes

If you're having trouble with a word in the question or answer choices, try dissecting it. Take advantage of every clue that the word might include. Prefixes can be a huge help. Usually, they allow you to determine a basic meaning. *Pre-* means before, *post-* means after, *pro-* is positive, *de-* is negative. From prefixes, you can get an idea of the general meaning of the word and try to put it into context.

✓ Hedge Words

Watch out for critical hedge words, such as *likely, may, can, often, almost, mostly, usually, generally, rarely,* and *sometimes.* Question writers insert these hedge phrases to cover every possibility. Often an answer choice will be wrong simply because it leaves no room for exception. Be on guard for answer choices that have definitive words such as *exactly* and *always.*

✓ Switchback Words

Stay alert for *switchbacks.* These are the words and phrases frequently used to alert you to shifts in thought. The most common switchback words are *but, although,* and *however.* Others include *nevertheless, on the other hand, even though, while, in spite of, despite,* and *regardless of.* Switchback words are important to catch because they can change the direction of the question or an answer choice.

⊘ FACE VALUE

When in doubt, use common sense. Accept the situation in the problem at face value. Don't read too much into it. These problems will not require you to make wild assumptions. If you have to go beyond creativity and warp time or space in order to have an answer choice fit the question, then you should move on and consider the other answer choices. These are normal problems rooted in reality. The applicable relationship or explanation may not be readily apparent, but it is there for you to figure out. Use your common sense to interpret anything that isn't clear.

Answer Choice Strategies

⊘ ANSWER SELECTION

The most thorough way to pick an answer choice is to identify and eliminate wrong answers until only one is left, then confirm it is the correct answer. Sometimes an answer choice may immediately seem right, but be careful. The test writers will usually put more than one reasonable answer choice on each question, so take a second to read all of them and make sure that the other choices are not equally obvious. As long as you have time left, it is better to read every answer choice than to pick the first one that looks right without checking the others.

⊘ ANSWER CHOICE FAMILIES

An answer choice family consists of two (in rare cases, three) answer choices that are very similar in construction and cannot all be true at the same time. If you see two answer choices that are direct opposites or parallels, one of them is usually the correct answer. For instance, if one answer choice says that quantity *x* increases and another either says that quantity *x* decreases (opposite) or says that quantity *y* increases (parallel), then those answer choices would fall into the same family. An answer choice that doesn't match the construction of the answer choice family is more likely to be incorrect. Most questions will not have answer choice families, but when they do appear, you should be prepared to recognize them.

⊘ ELIMINATE ANSWERS

Eliminate answer choices as soon as you realize they are wrong, but make sure you consider all possibilities. If you are eliminating answer choices and realize that the last one you are left with is also wrong, don't panic. Start over and consider each choice again There may be something you missed the first time that you will realize on the second pass.

⊘ AVOID FACT TRAPS

Don't be distracted by an answer choice that is factually true but doesn't answer the question. You are looking for the choice that answers the question. Stay focused on what the question is asking for so you don't accidentally pick an answer that is true but incorrect. Always go back to the question and make sure the answer choice you've selected actually answers the question and is not merely a true statement.

⊘ EXTREME STATEMENTS

In general, you should avoid answers that put forth extreme actions as standard practice or proclaim controversial ideas as established fact. An answer choice that states the "process should be used in certain situations, if..." is much more likely to be correct than one that states the "process should be discontinued completely." The first is a calm rational statement and doesn't even make a definitive, uncompromising stance, using a hedge word *if* to provide wiggle room, whereas the second choice is far more extreme.

✓ Benchmark

As you read through the answer choices and you come across one that seems to answer the question well, mentally select that answer choice. This is not your final answer, but it's the one that will help you evaluate the other answer choices. The one that you selected is your benchmark or standard for judging each of the other answer choices. Every other answer choice must be compared to your benchmark. That choice is correct until proven otherwise by another answer choice beating it. If you find a better answer, then that one becomes your new benchmark. Once you've decided that no other choice answers the question as well as your benchmark, you have your final answer.

✓ Predict the Answer

Before you even start looking at the answer choices, it is often best to try to predict the answer. When you come up with the answer on your own, it is easier to avoid distractions and traps because you will know exactly what to look for. The right answer choice is unlikely to be word-for-word what you came up with, but it should be a close match. Even if you are confident that you have the right answer, you should still take the time to read each option before moving on.

General Strategies

✓ Tough Questions

If you are stumped on a problem or it appears too hard or too difficult, don't waste time. Move on! Remember though, if you can quickly check for obviously incorrect answer choices, your chances of guessing correctly are greatly improved. Before you completely give up, at least try to knock out a couple of possible answers. Eliminate what you can and then guess at the remaining answer choices before moving on.

✓ Check Your Work

Since you will probably not know every term listed and the answer to every question, it is important that you get credit for the ones that you do know. Don't miss any questions through careless mistakes. If at all possible, try to take a second to look back over your answer selection and make sure you've selected the correct answer choice and haven't made a costly careless mistake (such as marking an answer choice that you didn't mean to mark). This quick double check should more than pay for itself in caught mistakes for the time it costs.

✓ Pace Yourself

It's easy to be overwhelmed when you're looking at a page full of questions; your mind is confused and full of random thoughts, and the clock is ticking down faster than you would like. Calm down and maintain the pace that you have set for yourself. Especially as you get down to the last few minutes of the test, don't let the small numbers on the clock make you panic. As long as you are on track by monitoring your pace, you are guaranteed to have time for each question.

✓ Don't Rush

It is very easy to make errors when you are in a hurry. Maintaining a fast pace in answering questions is pointless if it makes you miss questions that you would have gotten right otherwise. Test writers like to include distracting information and wrong answers that seem right. Taking a little extra time to avoid careless mistakes can make all the difference in your test score. Find a pace that allows you to be confident in the answers that you select.

✓ Keep Moving

Panicking will not help you pass the test, so do your best to stay calm and keep moving. Taking deep breaths and going through the answer elimination steps you practiced can help to break through a stress barrier and keep your pace.

Final Notes

The combination of a solid foundation of content knowledge and the confidence that comes from practicing your plan for applying that knowledge is the key to maximizing your performance on test day. As your foundation of content knowledge is built up and strengthened, you'll find that the strategies included in this chapter become more and more effective in helping you quickly sift through the distractions and traps of the test to isolate the correct answer.

Now that you're preparing to move forward into the test content chapters of this book, be sure to keep your goal in mind. As you read, think about how you will be able to apply this information on the test. If you've already seen sample questions for the test and you have an idea of the question format and style, try to come up with questions of your own that you can answer based on what you're reading. This will give you valuable practice applying your knowledge in the same ways you can expect to on test day.

Good luck and good studying!

Reading

Literature

Explicit Information

Explicit information includes facts and statements that are found directly in a passage or a story. It is not information that is hinted at or information you need to make a conclusion about. Explicit information may be found in many forms; it can be contained in a quote as well as in a description. It can be found in dialogue and in actions. This information can sometimes be used to support an inference. The answers to questions about explicit information are found through careful reading of the text. Attention is given to pertinent facts or other information. In fiction, details about characters, events, and setting can be both explicit and implicit.

Read the following excerpt and tell what information is explicit

> Carlos didn't really speak Spanish. His parents often spoke to him in that language, which he understood, but he always replied in English. As a result, his Spanish pronunciation was very bad, and he had trouble picking the right word. But then he fell in love with Alicia, who didn't understand English. Carlos changed very quickly.

The explicit information in the excerpt is all about Carlos. The passage says that he didn't really speak Spanish. It says that while his parents spoke to him in Spanish and that he understood it, he always responded in English. It also says his Spanish pronunciation was bad and he didn't pick the right words. This is explicit information. So is the fact that Carlos fell in love with Alicia and that Carlos changed quickly.

Inference

An inference is the best guess a reader can make based on the information in a passage. An inference has to be based on what a reader knows from personal knowledge and what is stated in a passage or story. Inferences can be about people, things, or ideas. A good inference is supported by information and is the most likely conclusion that can be made based on the evidence in a story or text. Inferences are not like explicit information, which is clearly stated in a passage. A reader must put the hints together to come up with the best conclusion to make a successful inference.

Read the excerpt and the question that follows it. Answer the question and explain why it is correct.

> The great day had arrived and Jesse could hardly believe it. For a whole year he had saved. All through the winter and spring he had worked overtime. Now it was June 25 and he was on his way. He would have two full weeks in Paris.

Tell why you can conclude that Jesse is going on vacation.

You can draw the conclusion that Jesse is going on a summer vacation because the information in the passage says that the great day had arrived and that Jesse had saved for this a whole year. It also says he would have two full weeks in Paris. This is a logical conclusion based on the information in the passage. It is the best guess a reader can make from the information that he or she has read. Inferences are based on the information in a passage and they are the best guess that a reader can make based on that information

Determining the Purpose of a Text

It should be, for the most part, fairly easy to determine the purpose of a text. When reading, ask yourself whether the passage is teaching or instructing you about something, trying to appeal to your emotions, trying to convince you of something, or simply trying to entertain you. There are certain signs that a text is attempting to persuade the reader. The author will offer up an opinion and tell why she thinks this way. If a text is simply informative, it will have many facts that will give details about an event or person, but will not offer an opinion. Examples of texts that entertain are novels, short stories, and science fiction. Instructional manuals that come with equipment are clearly not persuasive.

Determining the Theme of a Passage

The theme of a passage is the message or broad idea of the passage. It is what the passage teaches the reader. It is the lesson or moral that the passage carries with it. The theme of a passage is often based on one of life's universal themes. Most themes are about life, society, or human nature. A theme is not usually stated explicitly. The reader must figure it out from the topic, information, or plot of a passage. The theme is often why a passage is written. It helps give a passage unity. The theme is created through the development of the story. The events of a story help shape the kind of theme the passage teaches. Oftentimes, the author does not tell you what the theme is. You have to figure it out.

Read the following and decide which represents the best theme of the excerpt.

> Jeanie arrived at the bake sale early. She bought the biggest cake at the sale. Sally had to work late. When she finally got to the sale, no cakes were left. She got only two cookies. She was lucky to get anything.

Tell why "The early bird gets the worm" describes the story's theme best.

This saying is the closest to the theme of the story. In the story we read that Jeanie arrived early at the bake sale and got the biggest cake. But when Sally arrived, all that was left were two cookies. The point of the story is that the early bird gets the worm—the worm in this case is a large cake. The theme is what the story is teaching the reader. It is the message the author wants to get across. This is the message of this passage. The reader needs to figure out the theme from what happens in a story.

Creating an Objective Summary of a Passage

A summary must include the main ideas of a passage as well as the important details that support the main idea. It should be more than a general statement about what a passage is about. It should include vital events and other details that make the story unique and memorable. In order to make the summary objective, you must make sure to reflect what the passage is about. A summary puts the information in a short form. That is how summarizing is different from paraphrasing. Paraphrasing rewords the main idea and supporting ideas in greater detail; summaries do not. Summaries allow the reader to remember the main points of a passage and the important details.

Shaping a Character with Setting or Plot

Setting or plot shapes character because each helps to define the situation that a character finds herself in. A character is limited to the setting of a story. For example, if a story takes place in a cold environment filled with snow and ice, this is certain to impact what actions a character can and will undertake. Similarly the plot influences a character. What happens in the story directly affects what a character will do and how he will respond. For instance, if a character is faced with hardships, the way in which he deals with them will define who he is. That is why setting and plot are important to character development. No story is complete without either one.

Read the excerpt:

> She had swum too far out. The waves were higher than she thought. She was struggling hard to get to shore. She wondered if she would make it. She thought of her childhood. Had she been right to run away from home, she wondered? Just then, a lifeguard grabbed her and helped her to shore.

How the setting influences the character in this excerpt.

The setting of the ocean and the high waves creates a conflict in the character. She is worried. She thinks about her childhood and her parents. She doesn't know if she will make it to shore. This is how the setting affects the character in this excerpt. Without the high waves and the struggle, she would not become so worried and start to think about her past. She probably would not have questioned herself. This is an example of how a setting influences a character. If the waves had not been high, there probably would not have been a struggle or any self-searching of the swimmer's past.

Figurative use of a word or expression

Figurative language is a literary device. Figurative language allows the author to expand reality in a vivid way. When an author uses figurative language, she connects things in an exaggerated way in order to create a memorable image. Examples of figurative language are: simile; metaphor, personification, and hyperbole. Similes compare things using the comparing words *like* or *as*, for example, "Don swims like a dolphin." Metaphors compare things without using comparing words—for example, "Don is a dolphin in the water." Personification gives a thing or animal human traits—for example, "The water welcomed Don back." Hyperbole is an exaggeration that is not believable—for example, "Don swims a million laps in the pool every morning."

Read the excerpt from the poem.

> Roof-tops, roof-tops, what do you cover?
> Sad folk, bad folk, and many a glowing lover;
> Wise people, simple people, children of despair -
> Roof-tops, roof-tops, hiding pain and care.
> From "City Roofs" by Charles Hanson Towne

Tell what form of figurative language this is an example of and why.

This is an example of personification. In the poem, the poet asks the roof-tops, "what do you cover?" The poet is talking to the roof-tops as though they were people. In the excerpt, the roof-tops are treated like people; they are given human traits. This is the definition of what personification is. It is not an example of simile; there is no comparison using the words "as" or "like." It is not metaphor either because there is no comparison between two things sharing a similar quality. It is not an example of hyperbole; there is no exaggeration.

Difference between the denotative and connotative meaning of words

The denotative meaning of a word is the exact dictionary definition of the word. The connotative meaning of a word is what the word suggests. It is the emotion that is conveyed by the use of the word in context. The word may have associated meaning in addition to its dictionary definition. For example, the word "economical" is defined in the dictionary as saving money. But when the word is changed to "cheap" it takes on a different meaning, a more negative meaning. On the other hand, another synonym might be "frugal," which has a more positive meaning. Connotations are a subjective understanding of words. In such cases, the connotative meaning of a word in a passage can be found by looking at the context clues in the surrounding sentences.

READ THE FOLLOWING SENTENCE.

The outfit that Danae was wearing was not only attractive, it was stunning.

EXPLAIN THE CONNOTATIVE MEANINGS OF THE WORD "STUNNING" AND HOW IT RELATES TO THE WORD "ATTRACTIVE."

Both words, "stunning" and "attractive," mean "good looking." But the word "stunning" means that something is extremely good looking, so good looking as to catch someone's eye or stun a person. This word expresses a superlative rather than the word "attractive," which is less emphatic. Many things are attractive, but few are stunning. It is important to pick words that fit the situation, as this sentence does. Another word that means attractive is "cute," but as you can see, the connotations of this word are very different from "stunning." "Cute" means nice or pleasant, but it does not mean stunning, and yet both words mean attractive.

IMPACT OF RHYME AND OTHER REPETITIONS OF SOUNDS ON LITERATURE

Sound elements play with the way words sound. They are common in poetry and in spoken forms of writing like speeches and plays. For example, rhyme repeats the ending sound: "So very soon/We will fly to the moon" and is frequently used in poetry, mostly older forms of poetry rather than modern poems. Alliteration repeats beginning sounds, usually consonants: "Rah, rah, rah," the crowd cried, "rah, rah, rah." It is often used in spoken forms of writing as well as in poetry. Onomatopoeia uses a word that sounds like what it is: "Bees go buzz, buzz, buzz and snakes go hiss, hiss." It is often used in poetry for children.

EXPLAIN THE RHYME SCHEME OF THE FOLLOWING EXCERPT FROM A POEM BY EDGAR ALLAN POE.

ALONE - EDGAR ALLAN POE

From childhood's hour I have not been
As others were; I have not seen
As others saw; I could not bring
My passions from a common spring.
From the same source I have not taken
My sorrow; I could not awaken
My heart to joy at the same tone;
And all I loved, I loved alone.

The rhyme scheme that Edgar Allan Poe uses in this excerpt from his poem "Alone" is: a, a; b, b, c, c, d, d, e, e. Every two lines rhyme but the rhyme is not repeated in the other lines. This is a rather unusual rhyme scheme; many others have lines that repeat the rhyme scheme, but not in a consecutive order, such as a, b, a, b or a, b, c a, b, c. Rhymes are at the discretion of the poet, and are not mandatory. Many modern poems—actually, most of them—use a blank verse, where there are no rhyme schemes. There are many formal poetic types, such as the sonnet, that have a specific rhyme scheme that poets must follow to achieve that kind of poetic form.

SOLILOQUY

Soliloquies play a large role in shaping a play or drama because they allow the audience to have first-hand knowledge of what a character is feeling or thinking without having the interference of the other characters in the play. Soliloquies are really moments of the character being one on one with the audience. They are a chance for a character to bare his or her soul to the world in general. This experience creates an intensity of feeling between the character and the audience that leads to greater understanding of the character's personal plight and the meaning of the play. Such famous soliloquies as "To be or not to be" by Hamlet in the Shakespearean play of the same name live on because of the way in which they capture a human need to express doubt and a philosophy of life.

Poetic Form of a Sonnet Impacts the Meaning of Poetry

The sonnet is an important poetic form because it is a brief experience of what a poet is feeling or perceiving about life. Sonnets differ from other forms of poetry, such as odes or narrative poetry, because of these characteristics. The sonnet has a long history and was developed in Italy and then adapted by the British. Consequently, there are various forms of sonnets, but all sonnets have strict guidelines in terms of length and rhyme scheme. Sonnets are seen both as a challenge and as fundamental to poetry because of their brevity and lucidity. Shakespeare's sonnets are extremely famous and give a face to the playwright because they are so very personal. Most great poets have at one time or another used the sonnet for an expression of themselves and their lives.

Drama or Poem's Form Contributes to Its Meaning

The form or structure of a drama or poem is extremely important to the meaning of the text. There are many choices to be made when it comes to either form. Both poetry and drama come out of guidelines that were developed in Europe and England and then were brought to the United States, where they were used and sometimes changed to serve a different purpose. For instance, classically, the structure of a tragedy calls for a tragic or sad ending to the main character while a comedy never ends badly. However, both structures have been changed to meet the needs of modern society, and so today there are tragicomedies or comedic tragedies. The same is true of poetry. Strict rhyming poetry has given way to blank verse, for instance. And the choice of the structure of the poem or play gives the reader a hint as to its meaning.

Developing and Contrasting the Points of View of Different Characters or Narrators in a Text

An author uses many writing skills to develop a character's point of view in a piece of literature. By having a character respond to an event in a particular way, an author can show what the character thinks about it. Similarly, an author can choose to display a character's viewpoint through dialogue or actions. Various characters will have differing viewpoints and these can be shown in the conflict in a story or drama or even in a poem. Authors often display the narrator's point of view about characters, events, or the plot of a literary piece. The manner in which the author does this may be subtle or it may be overt. It is important to observe the language of the author, in order to analyze the author's and narrator's viewpoints about a character, an event, or a topic.

Read the Following Excerpt.

> Clarisse went to the window. She looked out. As was her habit, she dismissed the entire scene. To her it was no more than two people showing off. She failed to notice the severity of the matter, nor could she foresee the outcome of this untimely fight.

Analyze the Narrator's Viewpoint of Clarisse.

The narrator seems to have a rather dim view of Clarisse. She says that Clarisse dismissed the "entire scene" of the two people who were outside her window showing off. This seems to suggest that the narrator thinks she doesn't really relate to what is going on. The narrator also says that Clarisse "failed to notice the severity of the matter," which also suggests that Clarisse doesn't have a deep understanding of what is happening. From these comments, the reader can figure out that the narrator is not praising Clarisse, but instead is somewhat critical of Clarisse. When determining a narrator's viewpoint of a character, be sure to watch for clues that tell you the narrator's opinion, such as the clues in this excerpt.

Effects on a Written Piece of Literature When It Is Transformed into a Film or Multimedia Version of Itself

Modern films and multimedia versions of plays or other forms of fiction are indeed transformations of original pieces of literature. There are many parameters that will change the feeling, intent, intensity, and importance of the original work. They include the many technological advances that films and multimedia permit producers of such works. Many people read a book and then, when they see a movie based on it, are either happy with the outcome or upset. Lighting, sound, camera angles, whether or not the plot is followed closely, all affect the finished piece. While a balance between the original text and the move is preferable, this does not always occur because some producers prefer to use all that is available technologically, which may or may not prove fruitful. Certainly the interpretation of a piece of literature to film or video is something that must be considered on many levels.

Historical Fiction May or May Not Mirror Reality

Historical fiction often deviates from the historical reality in order to tell a story and make the historical event more moving to the audience. Historical fiction, while being accurate for the most part, may take poetic license when it comes to individual characters or the details of a situation. For instance, a story might take place during the American Revolution. While the author would most certainly have the details of when and where an event took place, the author might fictionalize a character that was not mentioned in the actual accounts of the battle. Or the author could take a person who was mentioned and turn this person into a character of his or her liking. When reading historical fiction, you need always remind yourself that all the details mentioned are not accurate; this is why it is called historical fiction rather than history.

Importance of Being Able to Read and Comprehend a Wide Variety of Texts That Are at a Specific Grade Level

It is important that a student be able to read and comprehend a wide variety of texts at a specific grade level in order to succeed in school and elsewhere. Being able to read a wide variety of texts will ensure an excellent vocabulary as well as an appreciation for literature and other topics. Reading has been proven to be the one sure way to improve general education on many levels. It will allow the student to increase his or her ability to grab the essence of a book and to grow a vocabulary for words, both in understanding meaning and in spelling. It will also improve a student's grasp of grammar, language conventions, and good writing skills.

Read the following soliloquy.

Time was that I was young, but now I am old and grey. No one sees me. No one hears me. It is age that they see, only age. This is my life for now. My youth is gone.

How does this soliloquy contribute to the meaning of a text or drama?

It explains how the character feels about growing old. It shows the inner thoughts of the character and what the character feels about himself. The speaker obviously does not like being old. The speaker thinks that he is no longer seen by the people around him. In other words the speaker feels useless to a large degree. The speech is also a commentary about society, that youth is the only force that is viable and that old age is not able to achieve anything that is meaningful. This is how the soliloquy would affect a text or drama.

Analyze the feelings in the excerpt of this sonnet by William Shakespeare.

How do I love thee? Let me count the ways.
I love thee to the depth and breadth and height
My soul can reach, when feeling out of sight
For the ends of Being and ideal Grace.

The poet is expressing his love for someone, and he uses language that shows that he loves the person very much. He loves to the depth, breadth, and height of his soul. This is very common in the sonnet form. It is often used to express the feelings of the poet. Sonnets are a form of poetry that many poets have used. Sonnets have very strict rhyme patterns and follow other guidelines. But they do allow the poet to express his or her own feelings, unlike other kinds of poems.

Describe the interaction between Melissa and Sam in the following passage.

> Melissa read Sam's report. She rolled her eyes. "You have no idea how to do this, do you?" Sam looked crestfallen.

The interaction between Melissa and Sam is that Melissa is criticizing Sam's report and Sam is upset by what she says. You can tell this from what Melissa says to Sam and the description of how Sam looks as he reacts to her words. It is important to analyze any reaction between people, events, or ideas when reading a passage. Besides fiction, there is a great deal of interaction between individuals, events, and ideas in an informational text. For instance, a persuasive passage will doubtless affect the reader because of the stance it takes on a particular subject. What the author says will have a reaction, whether it is positive or negative. There are interactions in other kinds of nonfiction as well. A text that covers a particular person or event will elicit feelings about what has been stated. For instance, in newspaper articles, people learn about people who have done newsworthy acts; they also read about events that are historic.

Informational Texts

Inference

Explicit information is information that is stated in a passage. It is stated right in the text; it is not suggested or hinted at. Explicit information can be facts or details about a topic. Frequently this information supports a main idea or thesis. Explicit information can be found just by reading a text, especially an informational passage. The explicit information in passages can, however, be used to form the basis for an inference. When making an inference, you need to put together the explicit information to form a conclusion. It is the best guess that a reader can make based on the information given in a passage.

Read the following excerpt. Tell whether it contains explicit information or not.

> I think the most famous person in the Old West is Annie Oakley. Annie is the best rifle shot who ever lived. She almost never missed. Many men challenged her to contests of speed and accuracy. She won them all.

Most of the information in the excerpt is explicit information. The information tells the reader about Annie Oakley: that she was the best rifle shot who ever lived and that she almost never missed. It also says that many men challenged her to contests and she won them all. This information is found right in the excerpt. It is not suggested or hinted at. Everything that is said is clearly what it means. The first sentence is a personal opinion; it is also explicit because the reader does not have to guess what the author thinks of Annie Oakley.

Read the passage.

> The Vikings set out in their boats in summer. The number of people in Scandinavia was growing fast. They needed to grow more food. In the late 900s, Eric the Red sailed across the Atlantic to Greenland. In 985, Viking farmers settled in Greenland.

Discuss why the conclusion that the Vikings were searching for new farmland is valid.

When you make an inference, you need to look at the information in the passage. The passage says that the Viking population was growing and that they needed to be able to grow more food. It is logical to guess that they sailed in search of new farmland. There is really not another possibility. Remember, inferences are assumptions that are hinted at or suggested by the text. They are not like explicit information; they are implicit in the text based on the explicit information that is found there. They are the best guess a reader can make.

Determining the Main Ideas of a Passage

Main ideas are what passages are mostly about. They are the important ideas that a reader comes away with after reading a passage. It is why the passage is written. Passages may have more than one main idea; paragraphs may have a main idea of their own, or the entire passage could have more than one main idea. What determines a main idea is that it is the far-reaching thought that the passage or paragraph is about. It is not a detail. Details in a passage or paragraph may support the main idea, that is, they tell more about the main idea, but they are not the main idea.

Decide what the main idea is of the passage that follows and why it is the main idea.

> You can save yourself a lot of money if you learn how to refinish furniture. When you refinish a piece of furniture, you get rid of all the marks and scratches that have accumulated over the years. Your furniture looks like new. You can also give it a different look by changing the color of the stain, paint, or varnish.

The main idea is that refinishing is a good way to improve old furniture. The author tells us ways that refinishing can improve old furniture. This is the main idea of the passage. Everything else in the passage is a supporting detail. Always make sure that when figuring out the main idea of a passage, you choose what the passage is mostly about, not what one section is about or something about the main idea. This passage is short, so there is only one main idea in it. When analyzing which statement is a main idea, make sure to choose one that has a broad message, not one that is talking about something specific.

Determining the Meaning of Words and Phrases from the Way They Are Used in a Text

The meanings of words and phrases can be determined from the way they are used in a text by using the context clues that are available in a passage. For instance, in the following sentences, there are context clues that help the reader understand the meaning of "cordial."

> The salesperson smiled when the couple came into the store. She told them to take their time in choosing a ring. She chatted with them about their future plans. She was the most *cordial* salesperson they had ever met.

From these sentences, the reader can figure out that the meaning of cordial is friendly. The salesperson smiled; she told them to take their time; she chatted with them. She was friendly. These are context clues that help the reader figure out the meaning of a word. The same can be done with phrases.

Read the sentence and explain the meaning of "sense of foreboding."

> All day long Ron kept thinking about Sue. For some unknown reason he was worried about her. He had a strong *sense of foreboding* that something was about to go wrong in Sue's city. Then he heard about the earthquake there. Luckily Sue was not injured.

To figure out the meaning of the phrase "sense of foreboding," the reader needs to look for context clues in just the same way the reader would do to figure out the meaning of a single word. The excerpt says that Ron was "worried" about Sue for "some unknown reason." It also says that he felt that "something was going to go wrong in Sue's city." Ron also heard about an earthquake taking place in Sue's city. A "sense of foreboding" must mean that Ron had an idea that something bad was going to happen. The context clues help the reader figure out the meaning of the phrase.

READ THE EXCERPT BELOW AND, USING CONTEXT CLUES, DECIDE WHAT THE WORD "DISBURSED" MEANS.

> It was May and Francesca hadn't received her insurance money. She wondered why it was taking so long. She needed the money to pay the contractor. When she called, a woman said that the money would be *disbursed* soon. That made Francesca feel better.

Using context clues is a good way to figure out the meanings of words and expressions without having to look them up in the dictionary. The way to discover context clues is to study the text. The excerpt says that Francesca had not received her insurance money for the hurricane's damage. It says that she had done the paperwork and that she needed the money to pay for the repair work to the house. Francesca felt a lot better when a woman at the insurance office said it would be disbursed by June 1. If you substitute the word "sent" for "disbursed," you can see that it makes sense. It fits with all the context clues and explains why Francesca would feel better.

FIGURATIVE LANGUAGE

Authors often make use of figurative language, which allows the writer to expand the way in which he or she uses language. Figurative language uses words in a non-literal way; this means that the word or expression takes on a new meaning. For instance, an author might say that Tom is like a robot. While everyone knows that Tom is a person, the image of Tom as a robot casts a new means of description. Figurative language takes many forms; it can be in the form of a simile, a metaphor, personification, or hyperbole. Similes compare things using the comparing word *like* or *as*—for example, "Tom is like a robot." Metaphors compare things without using comparing words—for example, "Tom is a robot when it comes to numbers." Personification gives a thing or animal human traits—for example, "The machine beckoned to Tom."

READ THE EXCERPT WRITTEN BY MARTIN LUTHER KING, JR.

> "One hundred years later, the Negro is still languishing in the corners of American society and finds himself an exile in his own land."

DISCUSS WHAT KING MEANS WHEN HE CALLS THE NEGRO "AN EXILE IN HIS OWN LAND."

Dr. King uses metaphors to express what he feels about the plight of the American Negro in this excerpt, especially in the metaphor where he likens the Negro to an exile in his own land. An exile is someone who is cast out, but in this case he is in his own land, so this is extremely sad and a very effective way of demonstrating the problems that African Americans were facing. Figurative language is a strong and effective way to get a point across, as in the case of this metaphor. Such a metaphor makes people sit up and listen to what is being said.

CONNOTATIONS OF THE WORD "RAGGED" AS COMPARED WITH THE EXPRESSION "WORN OUT"

The word "ragged" and the expression "worn out" both mean old and used, but "ragged" suggests something stronger. It suggests that the object is "in rags" and looking terrible; "worn out" merely means that something is old and used, but it does not suggest that it is in rags or terrible looking. Connotations carry many secondary meanings, so it is important to choose words that fit the situation. They are also filled with emotional meanings that should be analyzed and understood before choosing the word that you want to use. A dress may look worn out, but that dress probably does not look ragged. There is a difference in meaning, so it is important for the writer to choose the most accurate word.

DETERMINING THE STRUCTURE THAT AN AUTHOR USES IN A PASSAGE

There are basically seven different kinds of structures that are used in passages: question and answer order, chronological or sequential order, problem and solution order, cause and effect order, compare and contrast order, order of importance, and spatial order. There are often combinations of these structures in longer passages. Question and answer order opens with a question and then gives the answer; chronological order gives events in the order that they happen; problem and solution order offers a problem and then resolves it; cause and effect has a cause that results in a certain effect; compare and contrast is used to compare two ideas, things, or people; order of importance is self-explanatory; and spatial order is where a passage is ordered according to how something looks or where things are located.

TOM IS DOING A REPORT ON GOOD NUTRITION AND WHAT THE BENEFITS OF EATING RIGHT ARE. HE IS BEGINNING TO WRITE HIS ESSAY. DESCRIBE WHICH TYPE OF ORDER WOULD PROBABLY WORK BEST FOR HIS REPORT AND WHY.

The best choice would probably be a cause and effect organization for the report. A cause and effect order would allow the author to list the benefit of healthy eating and the effects of not eating well so that they would be easily comprehended by the reader. A compare and contrast order might also be considered, but if the emphasis is on the benefits of healthful eating, a cause and effect order would be more to the point and more effective. Obviously, a chronological order would have no place in the report, nor would a spatial order. The order an author uses is usually central to the topic the author chooses.

DETERMINING AN AUTHOR'S POINT OF VIEW

The author's point of view may be clear or it may be hidden. It is important to read a text closely to find out exactly what the author thinks about the event, person, topic, or issue that the author is writing about. When reading, look for clues to the author's viewpoint in terms of emotional statements or critiques of others discussing the topic. Some authors make their viewpoints very clear by stating it at the beginning of a text; but others want to keep their own opinions somewhat secret for many possible reasons. The author may not want to appear biased in one way or another and certainly some authors try very hard to stay objective. Still there are other authors who have a definite viewpoint but choose to conceal it and use other writers' comments to convey their own viewpoint. The reason it is important to ascertain an author's viewpoint is to ensure that you are reading something that gives a total picture of the topic, without bias.

READ THE FOLLOWING EXCERPT.

> Dear Editor: We must support the "Save-the-Buffalo" bill before Congress. Anyone with any concern about animal life and the environment must support this bill. The people who vote against it are selfish fools who don't care about the environment.

DESCRIBE THE VIEWPOINT OF THE AUTHOR AND TELL IF THE LETTER COULD BE IMPROVED.

The author of the letter's viewpoint is clear; he states what he thinks right away. He is in favor of the "Save-the-Buffalo" bill and he argues that people should support it if they care about the environment. He also insults those who are against by the bill by calling them selfish fools and saying they don't care about the environment. This letter is not subtle in any way. It is the complete opposite. The letter could be improved by the author using facts or figures to back up his argument rather than insulting those who do not agree with him.

EXPLAIN THE PURPOSE OF THE PASSAGE BELOW.

> The gray whale is a baleen whale; it has no teeth. Instead it has sieve-like plates that hang from the upper jaw to filter krill, plankton, and other small organisms from the sea water. The baleen plates are always wearing out and continue to grow throughout the whale's life.

This passage talks about baleen whales and gives details about them. There is nothing in the passage that tries to persuade the reader and there are no statements of opinion in the passage at all. Instead all of the statements are facts. This is what a passage does that has as its purpose to inform. It states details or facts about a topic. This passage is not funny, so it is not meant to amuse. The passage does not solve any problem, request anything, or narrate a story either. That is how the reader can tell that its purpose is to inform.

ORAL DELIVERY OF A TEXT WILL AFFECT ITS IMPACT ON A LISTENER

The written word becomes a completely different tool when it is spoken. Depending on the tone of the speaker, words take on new life and those that seemed to be benign may become strong statements that will propel the listener into action. Audio texts help listeners to hear the tone and intent of a speaker, but videos have an even greater impact because seeing a person speak is even more energizing (or not) than simply listening. The demeanor of the speaker can be analyzed and it will affect the way someone listening responds to a text. Consequently, multimedia versions are even more effective because they can add music, videos, or whatever effects a producer wishes to include. The multimedia versions of a text can have far-reaching effects, probably much more powerful than ever envisioned by the author of the text itself.

ASSESSING WHETHER AN ARGUMENT IN A TEXT IS SOUND AND VALID

When reading a persuasive text, it is important to analyze whether an argument is sound and valid and also whether the evidence that is given to support the argument is relevant and sufficient to support a claim. For instance, make sure to understand and research the topic of the passage and the opinions that the author is offering. Look at the supporting evidence and notice where it comes from. Is the evidence filled with opinions or is it based on facts? Are the facts from a source that is reliable or from a source that cannot be substantiated? Beware of claims that try to make a connection on an emotional level or arguments that tug at possible biases or prejudices. Make sure to reread the material more than once before taking any of the arguments or evidence seriously.

ANALYZING THE WORKS OF TWO OR MORE AUTHORS ON THE SAME TOPIC

When reading about a single topic that has been the subject of two or more texts, there are several things that must be done to compare them objectively. The reader needs to read each text carefully and take note of the point of view of the author as well as the reason the work was written. For instance, one author may be writing an opinion piece about a person and the person's beliefs, while a second writer may be doing an analysis of what the person has done and the kinds of issues the person is involved in. These two approaches could work to help the reader learn a great deal about a subject, from both a subjective and an objective manner. Another author might choose to write a biography about the same subject, which would lend more of an understanding of the person's life and those things that influenced her. When reading multiple texts about a single subject, it is wise to keep notes so that you can refer back and see the various ways in which one topic is presented. Reading more than one text on a subject certainly is a broadening experience.

IMPORTANCE OF BEING A PROFICIENT READER OF NONFICTION TEXTS

Being able to read a wide range of nonfiction texts is of extreme importance to a student, who needs to be able to learn as much as possible from the texts available to him or her. Whether it is a newspaper, an instructional manual, or a science text, it is extremely vital that a student feel at home and comfortable when reading and is able to comprehend the material without extreme effort. Without this ability, a student will not meet with success in the various fields that she will encounter as she proceeds through school and through life. The ability to read nonfiction is essential to success in the business world as well as the academic field.

Writing

PRODUCING CLEAR AND COHERENT WRITING

The first step to producing clear and coherent writing is to plan first what you are going to say, how you want to say it, and who your audience is. Think about the tone you want to project. While writing, develop and organize arguments in a logical order. Thoughts should be organized into paragraphs. Sentences should be precise. Support ideas with evidence, and mention opposing points of view as well. Then follow up with a conclusion. Be careful of too much repetition and use punctuation correctly to emphasize points. After writing, check for errors, both mechanical and in content, and make necessary revisions. Many find it useful to read the text aloud as a final guidepost.

CONSTRUCTIVE CRITICISM

A process of ongoing, constructive criticism of previous work from peers and adults in the classroom can help you improve your writing. It is often easier for others to see what needs to be improved than for the writer himself. Having a brief plan in mind before starting to write is useful, so that you know what points you want to cover. After completing your writing, leave it alone for a while. When you look at it again, your mind will be much fresher. Revising your writing means rethinking it; ask yourself if the reader will understand what you are trying to say. Did you achieve your purpose? Editing involves looking for better use of vocabulary, grammar, and sentence structure. Then the process of rewriting begins. At that time, it is possible that you may decide to try another approach. You may need to revise your main idea and make the supporting details clearer. Make sure that your work will create interest in the audience that you will choose. Ask for help from appropriate adults to review and critique or correct your text.

CONDUCTING A SHORT RESEARCH PROJECT

When conducting a short research project to answer a question, start by making a list of key words that relate to the question at hand. These words will be used by a search engine to begin the search for information. The words can also be used when utilizing an encyclopedia, either in print or online, or searching through back issues of journals, magazines, or newspapers. Whatever the source of the information, make sure it is timely and not dated. The sources that are used should be cited properly, following the standards of the Modern Language Association (MLA).Questions that are posed in the research project should be clear and explicit. Use the information that you have researched to expand your investigation by creating other focus questions.

USING THE INTERNET

There are many electronic sources now available for students to get written works of all kinds published online at no cost. Technology also allows for easy access to sources used in a writing project. These sources can be cited by listing the URL, title, author, and date retrieved. The growth of chat rooms and topic websites now allows for an unprecedented exchange of information. In addition, many free tools are accessible that provide software to allow people to work together on all kinds of projects, no matter how far apart they are geographically. Students can find discussion groups, file sharing networks, social networking sites, blogs, and task management sites, all of which foster interaction and collaboration.

GATHERING RELEVANT INFORMATION FROM MULTIPLE PRINT AND DIGITAL SOURCES

Gathering relevant information from multiple print and digital sources requires judging, first of all, how much information is necessary for the size of the project. The researcher should then think about how knowledgeable her audience is on the subject. While researching, it is important to maintain a balance between being too specific, with unnecessary details, and being too general, with oversimplifications. It is also important to check the age of the source material. There are many sources a researcher can turn to the Internet, journals, newspapers, text books, even works by other students, to name a few. Using search engines makes the task easier; generally one query will bring up all the data needed. Plagiarism, or using another's words without any acknowledgment, can be avoided by giving credit to works cited using MLA (Modern Language Association) standards.

Historical Fiction

Historical fiction can often stray from historical reality in order to tell a story and make the historical event more interesting to the reader. While being true for the most part, historical fiction may take poetic license when it comes to individual characters or the details of a situation. For instance, a story might take place in 19th-century Britain. While the author would have the details correct as to when and where an event took place, the author might fictionalize a character that did not actually live during this period. Or the author could take a person who was mentioned in research and turn this person into a character of his or her liking. When reading historical fiction, you need to always remind yourself that all the details mentioned might not be accurate; this is why it is called historical fiction rather than history.

Reading Literary Nonfiction

Reading literary nonfiction works requires digging for the author's point of view. You need to use critical thinking skills to determine whether the reasoning is sound. Ask yourself whether you can discern what the central idea of the passage is. Does the language seem confident and persuasive? Can you distinguish between what is fact and what is opinion? Look for statistics and representative examples to back up arguments and support the author's claims. Look for evidence of bias, omissions, and stereotypes; their presence severely limits the relevance of the work. Check sources to make sure that the information is timely.

Make Writing a Habit

Writing is important in all aspects of adult life. Therefore, it is important to learn to write routinely so that writing comes easily and smoothly. Teaching yourself that writing can be a habit means that you will understand that the more often you write, the better your writing will become. Once you understand the process of writing (making notes, drafting, writing, editing, revising), you will understand the concept of writing for different kinds of audiences and writing longer, more thoroughly researched articles as well as shorter, quick articles, and you will understand that some topics require much more effort and time than others. Learning the skills necessary to master the art of writing for specific disciplines leads to greater recognition in any field you choose.

Analyze the claim made in the statement below.

> The Good Value Supermarket should be closed. It has been cited numerous times for failure to live up to cleanliness standards. I have been to the market and seen firsthand examples of unclean practices. We should act at once.

The claim may or may not be valid. While the statement says that the market has been cited numerous times for failure to live up to cleanliness standards, it does not give a source for this claim, which lessens its import. The statement then includes a firsthand account, which may or may not be accurate and then resorts to an emotional plea, neither of which strengthen the claim. When making a claim, the argument should be well researched, and sources should be used to back up the claim and make it a valid one. This is not the case in the statement that was given.

TELL WHICH OF THE FOLLOWING WORDS FITS BEST IN THE BLANK AND WHY: "BECAUSE" OR "OTHERWISE."

The lawyer tried to prove his client was innocent; ___he would go to prison.

"Otherwise" is the correct choice because it creates a relationship of contrast. The word "because" suggests a cause and effect relationship, which does not exist in the sentence. The same is true of the word "since." It is important to understand the relationship between what might happen and what is happening in order to ensure that your sentences have a logical flow. Here the relationship that exists is between opposing possibilities. Cause and effect relationships indicate what will happen as a result of something taking place, which is not the case here. With the addition of the word "otherwise," there is a natural, logical flow in the sentence.

HAROLD WAS WRITING A PRESENTATION ON THE REASONS THAT SCHOOLS SHOULD REQUIRE UNIFORMS. HE NEEDED A CLOSING STATEMENT. DESCRIBE HOW HE SHOULD GO ABOUT WRITING A CONCLUSION.

He should review all of the arguments that he has made for requiring uniforms and then he should make a general final statement about why he feels it would be a good idea. He can use a personal appeal here and hope that the reader will agree with his point of view. It is probably best not to include opposing points of view in the conclusion. The conclusion that Harold writes should sound like the ending of the presentation. It should not introduce new material or leave items open for further discussion.

HERE IS THE BEGINNING OF A REPORT THAT BRAD IS WRITING. DISCUSS HOW TO IMPROVE IT.

Bats are interesting animals. They have wings. They eat insects. I saw a bat once when I was camping in the woods. We went into a cave and there were a lot of them sleeping.

This beginning is not very strong. It starts out with a statement, then has two facts about bats, but then goes into a personal accounting of when the writer saw a bat. The opening of a report should have a broad statement about the topic and then discuss what areas of the topic will be covered in the report. Personal accounts usually have little place in a formal report that is supposed to be based on a person's research, although a personal account might be a way of making the topic more interesting to the reader. But it does not take the place of solid research.

DECIDE WHICH EVENT HAPPENS FIRST.

MARGO WAS FALLING INTO A POOL OF WATER. OR WAS SHE FLYING IN THE SKY? MAYBE SHE WAS A DRAGON. SHE COULDN'T BE SURE. SHE THOUGHT ABOUT WHAT HAD HAPPENED EARLIER. SHE ATE THE STRANGE CANDY AND SHE FELT GIDDY. WHAT WAS HAPPENING TO HER? SHE HAD NO IDEA.

It is important to figure out the sequence of events in order to grasp what is happening in the passage. It says that Margo was falling into a pool of water and then it says that she was flying in the sky. Then it says she may have been a dragon. But the key to the sequence is in the word "earlier": "She thought about what had happened earlier." This tells us that the next event was the first in a progression of events. She ate the candy first. Then she felt giddy. So the reader can figure out the sequence of events and then better grasp the meaning of the story.

Persuasive text

INTRODUCING ARGUMENTS

When introducing arguments for or against a claim in a persuasive text, be sure that the argument is thoroughly researched and thought through. Make sure to organize your argument; the best way to do this is to make notes or an outline. Put the claim first and then list the reasons and evidence that you have to support the claim. Make sure the reasons and evidence follow from each other so that they are in a logical order. Delete any reasons or claims that cannot be substantiated by outside sources. By doing this you will be prepared to make a presentation that is compelling and convincing.

Making a Claim

When making a claim, you will need to research arguments in support of it that come from trustworthy sources. It is not enough to research a claim on the Internet because many sources are doubtful. You will need to find information that can be verified by several objective sites if you are doing research on the Internet. Another avenue is to find authorities in a field who have written or spoken on the topic that you are presenting so that you can quote these people. These authorities should have substantial degrees in their field as well as a vast experience so that their opinions will have credence and respect. Be sure to cite any information that you use to support a claim correctly. And make sure to present your arguments in a logical manner so that they will be easily understood by the listener or reader.

Creating Cohesion

When writing, it is important to phrase your sentences so that they follow logically and so that the claim and the evidence are clearly identified and related. Words or phrases such as "because," "since, "as a result of," and "as a consequence" or "consequently" all suggest a causality that may exist between a reason and a claim. Clauses can also be utilized to show relationships. "Because the temperature of the water is lower, the fish become dormant" shows causality between the reason and the effect. When writing, make sure to recheck your sentences to ensure that there is a natural flow and that relationships between causes and effects are evident and logical.

Formal Style

When writing a persuasive essay or other kind of formal paper, a formal style needs to be maintained throughout. The requirements of a formal writing style include the use of the third person, rather than first or second person. This lends a more serious tone to a paper and keeps personal feelings from affecting the integrity of the text. A formal style also requires proper English conventions as well as language that is professional and without prejudice. A formal style does not allow for colloquialism or a casual conversational tone. It requires that the author remain at all times objective, giving a presentation that is based on logic and reason.

Read the following passage. Suggest how to make it more formal.

> I've read in magazines that there is a lot of talk these days about artificial sweeteners. It's hard to tell if they are good for you or not. I need to lose weight. Plus I'm worried I'll get diabetes. So I think I am going to try some.

The style of the passage is very informal and personalized; the first person is used exclusively. Sentences are all short and simple, and there is little substance.

Here is one way to rewrite it.

> There have been reports published recently concerning the use of non-carbohydrate synthetic sugars, and the controversy that surrounds whether or not these products constitute a health risk. Individual use has been shown to be prompted primarily by a desire for weight loss, as well as to deter the onset of type 2 diabetes.

To make the passage more meaningful and more authoritative, third-person narration is substituted. Complex sentences are utilized. A higher, more specific vocabulary level is introduced—instead of *artificial sweeteners,* the substance is labeled scientifically: *non-carbohydrate synthetic sugars.* The result is that the passage is more authoritative. The information is presented in a more formal, structured manner.

IMPORTANCE OF HAVING A CONCLUSION

It is imperative to have a conclusion to any written or spoken presentation that sums up the overall intention of the text and gives the audience a sense of closure. The conclusion of a persuasive text should review the most important points that have been made in the presentation and the reasoning and arguments that the author has made to support them. The conclusion should not make the reader feel that there is more information to follow, but rather set the tone for the ending of the argument by being reassuring and providing an ending to the theme of the text. A good conclusion is important to the effectiveness of a text.

Informational or Explanatory Text

INTRODUCING A TOPIC

When writing an informational or explanatory text, the author will need to introduce the topic that the text will be about. This can be done in a number of ways. Often the topic is introduced as a topic sentence with supporting details coming after it. Very frequently authors attempt to find a way to make the topic relevant to what is going on in the modern world, even if the topic refers to something that is in the past, so that it will be immediately interesting to the reader. Along with introducing the topic, the author should preview the ideas and concepts that will be discussed by showing how relevant they are to the main topic. Many authors preview these concepts by showing how they affect everyday life. This also makes the text more relevant to the reader.

DEVELOPING A TOPIC

When an author develops a topic in an informational or explanatory text, the author must use relevant facts that will act as supporting details to the main topic. The topic may be included in a topic sentence and then followed by supporting details. These supporting details should be concrete facts that have been researched and are accurate. In addition to facts, it is a good idea to use quotes from experts in a field that is relevant to the topic. This will lend even greater meaning as well as interest for the audience. Examples, charts, and multimedia techniques will also enhance the presentation, but take care that the multimedia techniques support the main idea and are not a substitute for supporting details.

ANALYZE THE BEGINNING OF THIS INFORMATIONAL TEXT AND TELL HOW TO IMPROVE IT.

> Some people think that boys and girls should go to different schools. They give several reasons for this opinion. Girls participate more when boys aren't around. Boys and girls concentrate better when the opposite sex is not around.

This seems like a good start to an informational text. The first sentence sets out the topic. It tells what the report is going to be about. It also includes two supporting details to tell more about the topic. This is one way to introduce and develop a topic in a report or other informational or explanatory text. What should come are more supporting details and also sources for the information that is cited; this would make the report stronger and give it credence.

ORGANIZE IDEAS

There are numerous ways to organize the ideas that are presented in an informational or explanatory text. Certainly it is important to provide any definitions of concepts that might be unknown to the audience, but then the author needs to decide how to organize the material. Some authors choose to classify material; others prefer to use a compare and contrast or cause and effect organization. Whatever the organization that is chosen, the author may also opt to use headings and graphics, such as charts and/or tables. Multimedia alternatives, including audios and videos, can supply a range of ways to present new material that will be appealing to the audience as well as being effective.

READ THE FOLLOWING PASSAGE. EXPLAIN WHICH ORGANIZATION PATTERN WOULD SEEM TO BE THE BEST CHOICE AND WHY.

> Anita is writing an essay on crocodiles and alligators. She has compiled a long list of what they look like, what they eat, where they live, and who their predators are. She is unsure of how to organize her report.

A compare and contrast order would seem to be the best idea, since she would very easily be able to compare the ways the crocodiles and alligators look, what they eat, where they live, and who their predators are . The compare and contrast order works best when an author is writing about two animals, things, or people, since it allows the information about each one to be compiled in an orderly way that would be easy for the reader to understand. In addition to the order, Anita could use headings and charts to further organize the material. Audios and videos might also be a good supplement to the essay.

USING APPROPRIATE TRANSITIONS

When writing an informational or explanatory text, it is important to use appropriate transitions that will give cohesion to the text and also help clarify the relationships among ideas and concepts. For example, make sure to use transition words or phrases, such as "therefore," "consequently," and "as a result of," to show causality between ideas. Words such as "however," "on the other hand," "but," "in contrast," and "similarly" show a comparison and contrast relationship. Transition words and expressions that show examples include "for example," "for instance," "namely," and "that is." The order of importance can also be shown through transitions, such as "at first," "former," "latter," "primarily," and "second."

USING PRECISE LANGUAGE AND DOMAIN-SPECIFIC VOCABULARY

When writing informational or explanatory texts, it is vital to use precise language and domain-specific vocabulary to put forth your thesis and related ideas. Generalized vocabulary will do little to bring the points that you are making home to the audience, since they will not accurately reflect your thesis or supporting details. Domain-specific vocabulary is important to utilize because it will accurately describe or explain the ideas or processes that you are addressing. When you research a subject, make sure to familiarize yourself with any vocabulary that is involved in its explanation. Use dictionaries, if necessary, a technical dictionary, to decode any words you are not familiar with as well as context clues.

ESTABLISHING AND MAINTAINING A FORMAL STYLE

When writing an informational or explanatory text, it is important to establish and maintain a formal style of writing. Do not use a colloquial or casual tone. It is necessary to use the third person and to make the sentences longer and more complex. It is also important not to use any contractions when you write. A formal style announces that the writer is serious about his or her subject and wants to do it justice by keeping the thesis and supporting details clear, to the point, but as complex as they need to be. A formal style also means that the writer will not be interjecting a personal opinion that is not justified.

IMPORTANCE OF A CONCLUDING STATEMENT

A concluding statement or section that follows from and supports the information or explanation is important to a text, be it informational or explanatory because the conclusion helps to focus the important points in a text and also provides closure to the reader or audience. A good conclusion attempts to "wrap up" the passage so that the audience is made aware of a logical ending to the thesis. Without an effective conclusion, the passage would not have the weight it needs to have an impact. The conclusion should not make the reader feel that there is more information to follow, but rather set the tone for the ending of the argument by being reassuring and reiterating the important parts of the passage.

Narratives

Establishing a Point of View

When writing a narrative, a story line or plot should be conceived that will allow for a narrator and characters as well as the point of view of the narrator as well as the author. The author's viewpoint will not necessarily be the same as the narrator's viewpoint. Points of view can be shown through dialogue or the way the narrator reacts to what characters do in the story. The characters will need to be drawn very clearly through both their descriptions; the author can hide his point of view in the characters' thoughts or actions. The narrator's point of view is usually more overtly seen in what is said in the narrative by the narrator.

Discuss the character and point of view in the following passage.

> The mouse ran though the hole. She saw the cheese. She grabbed it, but then she heard noises. She couldn't make it back to the hole. She was terrified. She ran under a chair and remained there until it was quiet. Then she ate the cheese.

The author has chosen to tell the narrative from the point of view of the mouse. This makes the mouse more human and more attractive to the reader. The author gives the mouse human characteristics; the mouse feels and can also reason. The author has created a character out of the mouse by concentrating on it and telling what it does. This is one way an author can establish the point of view of a character in a narrative. It is not clear what the point of view of the author is, but this could come later in the narrative.

Sequence of Events

Sequence of events in a narrative should come naturally and logically out of the action and the plot. Rather than being forced, the sequence should follow the natural flow of a dialogue or plot and enhance what happens in the story. The only time that sequence is bypassed is when an author decides to use a literary device such as a flashback, which means the action does not flow in sequence but rather jumps back and forth. Events in a narrative are extremely important in helping the reader understand the intent or message of a narrative. When reading a narrative, take note of the order in which events occur to give a broader understanding of the passage.

Techniques Used by the Author

There are many techniques that authors employ to make their narratives come alive and have meaning. Among them, dialogue is an important factor, since it not only lets you know what is happening in a narrative, but it also colors what a character is like. The reader can tell from what a character says and how the character says it what the character feels about the events in a narrative. Equally important is the pacing that an author employs in revealing the nature of the characters and the kind of plot that is unraveling. This helps color the experiences and events in a narrative and increases the sensitivity of the audience. A third technique that broadens a narrative is the use of descriptions that help you visualize a character, what is happening, and what the character is doing.

Importance of Transition Words

Use of transition words are very important when writing a narrative. They can color the plot and the characters. They can also indicate the passage of time or the sequence of events. Sequence words, such as "first," "second," and "last," assist the reader in understanding the order in which events occur, which can be important to the flow of the plot. Words such as "then" and "next" also show the order in which events occur. "After a while" and "before this" are other sequence expressions. A change in setting can also be indicated. For instance, a passage may say, "First we went into the living room to talk," but later on it might say, "after we chatted for a while, we went into the dining room." This shows a shift in setting. When reading, notice transition words and their effect on the action.

Importance of Language

How language is used is extremely important in a narrative. Precise language can help a reader gain an insight into character through a description. Details of what characters do and the setting or events in a narrative are also important and should be written in as lively and thought-provoking a manner as possible. Sensory language helps convey the mood and feeling of the setting and characters and will bring insight into the theme of a narrative. When reading, take special care to understand the range of language that an author employs in order to better comprehend the meaning of a narrative.

Role of a Conclusion

The conclusion to a narrative is of the utmost importance, and without it a reader may end up feeling somewhat cheated by the experience of reading a story. The conclusion to a narrative is the resolution of the problem that is faced by the characters. The conclusion may not always be clear cut; it may leave some questions unanswered. But the conclusion should give the reader the sense that the narrative is over, whatever the outcome. Traditionally, in tragedies the conclusion is one of sadness. On the other hand, in comedies the conclusion is light-hearted. In modern literature, conclusions can be much more evasive than they are in traditional literature, which leaves the reader often with more questions than answers.

Describe what he should look for when trying to come up with a good conclusion.

> Charles is writing a short story about a girl running for school president. He writes about all that she has done to win the election. Now he is looking for a conclusion to his story.

Charles should look for a conclusion that brings the story together. If the story is about a girl running for school president and what she has done to win the election, it probably should conclude with whether she won the election or not. There are other possibilities also, but this is the most obvious conclusion that the story should have. A conclusion should bring the entire story to a fitting and appropriate ending so that the reader has a sense of closure. It should follow the opening and the many events that happen, so that there is a form to the story.

Speaking and Listening

Discussions

PREPARING FOR A DISCUSSION

Class discussions are important because they help prepare students for the importance of discussion in later life and allow them to practice effective techniques and learn skills as communicators. When preparing for a class discussion, it is necessary to do your homework and research the subject at hand. Make sure you have read all the information applicable and done all the necessary research. Have whatever resources (quotes, statistics, and audiovisual material) you need at hand. Rehearse your role; practice the day before with a family member or friend. Determine what you are going to focus on. If you are leading the discussion, think ahead about how you are going to guide the discussion to a conclusion and how long a time period will be needed.

RULES FOR COLLEGIAL DISCUSSIONS

Properly organized collegial discussions can be very productive and result in many new and interesting ideas being formulated and brought out in the classroom. Rules for participants should be set beforehand; roles for everyone need to be defined and clarified. Specific goals need to be established, and the progress toward reaching those goals should be tracked, with a deadline in mind for completion. Participants should learn how to use questions to add detail and depth to the discussion and how to build on and further ideas that are put forth by others. It is important to try to understand and communicate with individuals who have a different perspective, especially from a cultural point of view. Everyone should be able to make use of evidence and be able to express themselves clearly.

POSING QUESTIONS THAT ELICIT ELABORATION

Asking questions that encourage a response from others entails asking specific, not general, questions. Questions should force the listener to think. Questions should focus on how, what, and why. Questions should be open-ended, i.e., they can't be answered simply by a yes or no. It is important to be proficient at asking questions and at learning the art of asking the right question. Building on the ideas expressed by others in the classroom through intelligent questioning means learning the art of listening. Ask a question at the end, such as "Does that answer your question?" Personalize questions. And most importantly, take notes. Most people forget a surprising amount of what they hear. If others stray off the subject being discussed, bring them back by taking control of the situation and diplomatically steer the conversation back to the subject at hand.

ACKNOWLEDGING NEW INFORMATION

The first key to acknowledging new information in a discussion is careful listening. With careful listening, one can add clarity to the ideas already expressed and add depth to the material. The information should be acknowledged respectfully. Questions can be posed that include all the participants, so that all have an interest in, and respect for, the opinions of everyone involved. There should be an open exchange, so that constructive critiques of other points of view are encouraged and opinions can be modified based on the flow of questions and responses that arise. In this manner, new ideas will arise, and discussions will progress toward clarifying the topic(s) under consideration.

Analyzing the Main Ideas and Supporting Details in Diverse Media and Formats

Analyzing discussions utilizing graphics, images, and sound requires examining the overall effectiveness of the use of the diverse media in presenting the main points coherently. Does the use of the additional formats and media support the main idea, or does it detract from, even obscure, what the speaker is trying to express? Does the use of the media provide appropriate support to the purpose? The ideas presented in a discussion with diverse media can clarify the issue, provided there are no ulterior motives (i.e., political, social, or moral) in their use and that it does not result in claims that cannot be supported.

Analyzing a Speaker's Argument and Claims

The argument must be analyzed to determine if there is a clear delineation between evidence and theory. If a statement is theoretical, it needs to be identified as such so that it does not lead to confusion later on. Do the assumptions made by the speaker have too many generalizations? It is important that the argument provide sufficient evidence to convince the group of the validity of the claims being made. Are the speaker's arguments logical, and is the persuasion used intellectual, or emotional? Is there sufficient reasoning to support the claims? All facts and assumptions need to be tested, and the audience must understand the argument.

Claims and Findings Can Emphasize Salient Points in a Focused Manner

In a focused discussion, the attention paid to the details will result in a successful presentation, where the diverse partners in the group will come away with a feeling of having been present at something that was meaningful. Facts and examples should be stressed. Repetition creates retention. It is important that the speaker chooses the right words and builds momentum by leading up to the strongest argument(s) gradually. Graphics are important; participants will be more convinced if they can see evidence as well as hear it. By breaking up the flow of the discussion, using pauses before and after pertinent arguments, the speaker makes the presentation of facts more interesting.

Presentations

One of the most important tactics in an effective presentation during a discussion is eye contact. Maintaining eye contact with the other participants throughout a discussion ensures a presentation that is believable and, more than likely, a presentation with details that will be remembered. Merely reading a text will have little or no impact; looking into the audience's eyes will have a major impact. Smiling during the presentation of key points will attract the attention of the others in the classroom. Using clear diction, with a voice that is easily heard, and pronouncing words properly will also create an atmosphere of conviction when emphasizing main points.

The expression "a picture is worth a thousand words" is very true when making a presentation in a discussion. Graphics, diagrams, charts, and maps all serve to reinforce the point you are trying to make. The simpler they are, the more effective they will be. They serve to help the audience understand your argument. Spoken facts by themselves can be boring; using visuals helps to focus the audience and lessen the boredom factor. The same is true of using multimedia aids; a video or audio can enhance the claims and findings of a presentation. Both visuals and multimedia components should be considered as only aids; they are not going to do the work for you. It is useful to rehearse the presentation as many times as needed until it flows smoothly.

Stage presence is important when making a presentation. It requires a lot of practice beforehand, just as an actor has to learn her lines. The spoken presentation should include a variety of sentences, mixing simple, compound, complex, and compound-complex sentences as appropriate to maximize the development of salient points in the discussion without being pedantic. The words should flow naturally and not appear as though they are being read from a script. Eye contact should be made with the audience at all times. Maintaining a smile will help create an atmosphere of informality. Extra effort needs to be made to avoid being wordy. Redundancy is sure to make audience attention wander.

Language

Function of Phrases

A phrase is a group of words in a sentence which can act as a single part of speech. There are noun phrases and verb phrases. The additional words make the meaning more specific, so there are also prepositional phrases, appositive phrases, and absolute phrases. Phrases are not complete sentences because they lack either a predicate or a subject. Phrases are parts of sentences, and sentences are frequently made up of one or more phrases. An example of a phrase is "the white horse" or "went very quickly." As you can see, neither phrase is a complete sentence. The first phrase lacks a predicate and the second phrase lacks a subject.

Clause

A clause is a word group that has a subject and a predicate and is used by itself or as part of a sentence. Unlike a phrase, a clause can be independent or stand by itself. It can also be dependent, which means it doesn't stand on its own and depends on an independent clause. Dependent clauses begin with a relative pronoun such as: that, who, whom, whose, which, where, when, or why; or a subordinating conjunction, such as: after, because, if, since, unless, to name a few. Dependent clauses can act as nouns, adjectives, and adverbs. *"If we knew what it was we were doing, it would not be called research, would it?"* (Albert Einstein). In this sentence, "If we knew what it was we were doing" is a dependent clause acting as a noun.

Simple vs. Compound Sentence

A simple sentence has one main clause with one subject and one predicate and no dependent clauses, while a compound sentence has two or more clauses, often joined by a comma and a conjunction, and sometimes by a semicolon. The addition of various phrases can sometimes make a simple sentence appear compound, but if the sentence has only one main clause, it is a simple sentence: For example: *Children around the world love soccer.* (Simple) *Children around the world love soccer, and it is the world's most popular sport.* (Compound)

Complex vs. Compound-Complex Sentence

Adding dependent clauses to simple and compound sentences produces complex and compound-complex sentences. A complex sentence has one main clause and at least one dependent clause. A compound-complex sentence will have more than one main clause and at least one dependent clause.

"The path to my fixed purpose is laid on iron rails, on which my soul is grooved to run.'" (*Moby Dick*, Herman Melville) (Complex) *Although I love going to the movies, I haven't had very much time recently, and I don't know who to ask out.* (Compound-complex) It has two main clauses (I *haven't had much time, I don't know who to ask out)* and a dependent clause *(Although I love going to the movies).*

Identify what kind of sentence the following is and explain why this is true.

> George and his sister Veronica landed at the airport about 4:30 and left on the shuttle bus before we got there.

Many times looks can deceive. This is a simple sentence. There is one main clause. If it were a compound sentence, there would have to be two or more main clauses. It might be confusing because the simple subject and the simple predicate are expanded. It has a compound subject

(*George and his sister Veronica*), compound verb *(landed and left)*, adverbial phrase (*about 4:30*), and two prepositional phrases *(on the shuttle bus* and *before we got there*); therefore, despite the fact that it is a lengthy sentence, it is still just a simple sentence.

Describe how to rewrite the sentences below to include two dependent clauses.

I graduated from high school. I was given a hunting knife. My grandfather once owned it.

The sentences are all short and are all about the same topic. They can be put together to make a more interesting sentence that will contain the same information by using clauses. Here is one way a writer could change the sentences to improve the expression of the sentence.

After I graduated from high school, I was given a hunting knife that my grandfather once owned.

This revised sentence makes use of the dependent clause *After I graduated from high school* and the dependent clause *that my grandfather once owned* to make the passage more interesting to read.

Placing Phrases and Clauses Within a Sentence

Modifying phrases or clauses should be placed as closely as possible to the words they modify to ensure that the meaning of the sentence is clear. A misplaced modifier makes the meaning of a sentence murky. For instance, the meaning of *Walt barely missed the dog speeding down the street* becomes evident when the phrase is moved: *Speeding down the street, Walt barely missed the dog.* A dangling modifier doesn't have a word that it is modifying, so a word must be put into the sentence in order to complete its meaning. *Having arrived late for assembly, a written excuse was needed.* This sentence makes it sound as though the written excuse was late for assembly, so something needs to be added to the sentence. The meaning is clear when the name Jessica is added. *Having arrived late for assembly, Jessica needed a written excuse.* Here the phrase modifies Jessica.

Rewrite the following sentence so that it makes sense.

A poem which received little acclaim when he was alive, today readers all over the world enjoy reading Walt Whitman's Leaves of Grass.

In this sentence it is not clear what the clause *A poem which received little acclaim when he was alive* is actually modifying because *poem* is too far away from the title of the poem, *Leaves of Grass.* The reader is forced to pause and think about what the sentence means, so the writing is unclear. Rewritten as *Readers all over the world today enjoy Walt Whitman's Leaves of Grass, a poem which received little acclaim when he was alive* places the modifier correctly so that the reader can immediately grasp the author's meaning. It is important when writing to check for dangling modifiers.

Using Commas to Separate Coordinate Adjectives

Coordinate adjectives are adjectives that apply equally to the noun they precede, and each one should be separated by a comma. Adjectives are coordinate if it sounds right to put the word *and* between them or if it sounds right when the order of the adjectives is reversed. *It was an old, decrepit house.* When there are more than two coordinate adjectives, a comma goes before the conjunction *and. The children were tired, hungry, and happy.* Adjectives that are not coordinate are not separated by a comma. *The cracked front window needs to be replaced.* The adjective *cracked* modifies *front window,* and the sentence does not sound right as *The cracked and front window,* so a comma is not needed.

DESCRIBE HOW TO REWRITE THE FOLLOWING SENTENCES, USING COMMAS TO SEPARATE COORDINATE ADJECTIVES CORRECTLY.

Yesterday, the brothers went to the new, Westbrook dog show. Their favorite dog was a young, black Labrador named Ralph. It was an enjoyable exciting dog show, and they will definitely come again.

Correctly written, the sentences should read: *Yesterday, the brothers went to the new Westbrook dog show. Their favorite dog was a young black Labrador named Ralph. It was an enjoyable, exciting dog show, and they will definitely come again.* The adjective *new* modifies *Westbrook dog show* so a comma is not needed. The same is true of *young, black Labrador,* where the adjective modifies *black Labrador,* a specific breed. Notice it would not make sense to say *young and black Labrador,* or *black, young Labrador. Enjoyable* and *exciting* are coordinate adjectives and are correctly separated by a comma.

IDENTIFY THE INCORRECTLY SPELLED WORDS IN THE SENTENCE THAT FOLLOWS.

The information you have is not relible since it comes from a sorce that has not been investegated.

The words that are misspelled are "relible," which would be "reliable," "sorce," which is spelled "source," and "investegated," which is spelled "investigated." It is important to learn to spell words correctly. One way to learn how to spell words is to learn how to sound out words. Break longer words down into syllables and into affixes and roots. Get the correct spelling from a dictionary and then practice that spelling. Take on only a few new words at a time; go on to new words only when you are certain you have mastered the current group. Practice using your new words in sentences. And learn the basic spelling rules, most famously "*I* before *e* except after c" (receive) as well as "drop the final *e*" (like, liking) and "double the last consonant" (stop, stopped). 7.3

CONVENTIONS OF WRITTEN LANGUAGE

The conventions of written language dictate using capitalization and punctuation correctly. Proper names, the first word of a sentence, and titles should be capitalized. Also, the names of countries, rivers, and states are all capitalized. Correct punctuation means using end marks, commas, semicolons, colons, and apostrophes correctly. The conventions of written language also say an author should make sure each sentence is complete. There should not be run-on or sentence fragments. Good penmanship is also important, so that the reader can understand what has been written; handwriting should be neat. Spelling is another important part of the conventions of written language. Words should be spelled correctly. To accomplish this, it may be necessary to use a dictionary. By using these conventions, an author will be able to communicate more clearly.

DISCUSS WHY THE FOLLOWING SENTENCE DOES NOT USE THE APOSTROPHE CORRECTLY AND EXPLAIN WHY:

The puppy stopped it's whimpering when we got home.

The sentence uses an apostrophe incorrectly. No apostrophe is needed after "it" because "it's" is in a possessive form. As it is written here "it's" means "it is"; it is a contraction but it has no place in this sentence. When considering whether an apostrophe is correctly placed, always ask yourself whether the apostrophe takes the place of the word "of," because that is what the apostrophe indicates: *the clothing store of the women* or *the orders of the customers.* No possessive is indicated in the sentence as it is written. It would be different if the sentence said: The puppy's whimpering stopped. Then the possessive form is required, since it is the whimpering *of* the puppy.

Edit the following sentence so that it expresses ideas precisely and concisely, and wordiness and redundancy are eliminated.

> If you go to the library on Sunday, you will find the library doors are locked and that the facility is closed on Sunday.

This sentence can be written just as effectively as: "The library is closed on Sundays." The expression "the library doors are locked" is redundant; it is not needed. What the writer is really saying is that the library is closed on Sunday. The writer also repeats the word Sunday when it is unnecessary and makes the sentence wordy. When writing, reread and revise your text after writing to make it is concise and not redundant. When writing a paragraph, or a longer passage, make sure that your main point is prominent within the first two to three sentences. Use supporting details to express more information about the main idea. And be sure to include an opening and ending to your essay. The ending should review what your main idea is about.

Using Context Clues

The term *context clue* refers to the words or phrases built into the sentences surrounding a new word. They allow you to guess the meaning of the word. Context clues may include examples of the new word, synonyms, antonyms, definitions, or contrasting information. By using context clues in the surrounding sentences, the reader can figure out approximately what the word means. A context clue indicating an example may contain the words *including* or *such as* or have a dash or a colon before stated information. A synonym is a word meaning almost the same thing as the new word. An antonym is a word with the opposite meaning to the new word. A definition will state exactly what the new word means. Contrasting information will include facts that are different from the new word.

Using context clues, determine the meaning of "gregarious" in the following excerpt.

> Beverly is the most gregarious person I have ever known. She loves people and spends a lot of her time talking to her friends and arranging get-togethers. She doesn't mind spending hours cooking as long as she knows that her house will be filled with people.

The word "gregarious" means sociable—someone who likes to talk with other people is gregarious or sociable. The context clues tell you this is the word's meaning. The excerpt says Beverly loves people and spends a lot of her time talking with friends and arranging get-togethers. It also says that she likes her house filled with people. And the excerpt says that Beverly is the opposite of her sister, who does not entertain.

Explain how the context words in the following sentences are clues to helping understand the meaning of the underlined word.

> Emily was being very <u>blunt</u> with her brother. She didn't waste any time and came straight to the point.

There are numerous meanings to the word *blunt*. By reading carefully, you can figure out which meaning is appropriate here. The following sentence uses the phrases *waste any time* and *straight to the point*. These context clues support the fact that in this usage the word *blunt* most likely means short, curt, or even candid. It does not mean unsharpened or dull, which is another meaning of the word, because that would not make any sense; nor does it mean unfeeling, which is another common synonym, because that is not the sense that is being conveyed.

Knowledge of Affixes and Roots Can Be Helpful in Figuring Out the Meaning of a Word

A root word is the original word, before it is added onto. An affix is a prefix, infix, or suffix that is added onto a root word. Often, the affixes in the English language come from Latin or Greek origins. A prefix is added before a root word, an infix is added to the middle of a root word, and a suffix is added to the end of a root word. When you look at the meaning of a root word and the meaning of any affixes added to the root word, you can figure out the approximate meaning of the word. For example, the root word "like" means to enjoy. The prefix "dis-"means not. The reader can therefore see that "dislike" means to not enjoy.

The word "inscription" is made up of three sections. The root "script" means "write" or "writing." It comes from the Latin word *scribere,* meaning *to write*. There are two affixes in the word. The prefix *in-* can mean various things such as "not," but also "on." In this case it means "on." The suffix *-tion* means "action" or "process." So put together the word "inscription" means "the act of writing on." Studying roots and affixes is important because it allows you to decode words you might not otherwise understand with relative ease.

Using Specialized Reference Materials to Determine the Pronunciation of a Word

A print or digital dictionary can be used as a means to find the correct pronunciation of words. The dictionary will have a guide that shows how to sound out the words, the symbols used to indicate the sounds, along with sample sounds (like the "i" in "pie," for instance). The dictionary can also be used to determine the meaning of the word, as well as its part of speech. The thesaurus is useful because it lists synonyms for all the various meanings a word can have, to help you clarify the precise meaning as used in the context of the text you are reading. Many books will have a glossary, placed at the end of the book, to help you with difficult or unfamiliar words used in the text.

Melissa used her dictionary to check the various meanings of the word "counsel." She found this entry:

> coun•sel ('kaun(t) suhl) *noun* 1. advice asked for and given. 2. a consultation. 3. guarded or private thoughts. 4. a lawyer who advises clients 5. a consultant *verb* 6. to advise 7. to consult with someone

Explain the definition of "counsel" in the following sentence.

> He decided to counsel with an expert about his financial problems.

The correct answer is meaning 7, "to consult with someone." Meanings 1 and 2 are incorrect because these are nouns, neither is a verb, which is used in the sentence. Meaning 6 is the opposite of the meaning in the sentence. When considering which meaning is being used, always check for context clues in the sentence or in the sentences before or after the sentence in which the word is used. Dictionaries also tell you how to pronounce words and often give the derivation of the word, although it is not given here.

Discuss the meaning of the word "baffle" in the following sentence.

> The criminal tried to baffle the detective by creating false clues and putting misleading fingerprints on the weapon.

The word "baffle" in this sentence means to confuse. The context of the sentence helps the reader figure this out because the sentence says that the criminal tried to baffle the detective. If you replace the word "baffle" with "confuse," it makes sense. There are other meanings of the word "baffle," but they do not fit in the sentence. To figure out the meaning of the word, use the context clues and then check the meaning of the word in a dictionary, either in print or online. A dictionary will also help you determine the meaning of the word by saying what part of speech it is when used in a particular instance. In this case the word 'baffle" is used as a verb.

EXPLAIN WHAT FIGURE OF SPEECH IS USED IN THE FOLLOWING BIBLICAL PASSAGE AND WHAT IT MEANS:

"For all flesh is as grass, and all the glory of man as the flower of grass." (1 Peter 1:24)

There are many instances of figurative language in the Bible. Here, a simile is used to compare human life to grass. Man is not really like grass, but, just as grass, and the flower of grass, grows and dies, so too will man grow and die. You can spot the use of a simile because the word "like" or "as" is often used. Similes differ from metaphors because metaphors do not use the word "like" or "as" to make the analogy. Other kinds of figures of speech or figurative language are hyperbole and personification. Hyperbole is an exaggeration that cannot be believed. Personification gives objects and animals human characteristics.

USING THE RELATIONSHIPS BETWEEN WORDS TO BETTER UNDERSTAND THEM

You can use the relationships between words to figure out the meaning by looking at how the words are used in the context of the passage. When you see a word that you do not know, try to figure it out from context clues. Then try to think of a synonym that would make sense in place of the word. Also think of an antonym to help you clarify its meaning. Word analogies can help enhance a word's meaning as well. A word analogy exists when there is a similarity or agreement between two words or they have a relationship to each other. Word analogies serve to sharpen your thinking skills. Word analogies are written as "word 1 is to word 2 as word 3 is to word 4" or "word 1: word 2 :: word 3 : _____," where you need to pick the best choice of a word to fit in the blank space, depending on what kind of analogy it is. When trying to figure out a word analogy, think about the kind of relationship that exists between the first two words and then try to duplicate the relationship in the second pair of words.

DESCRIBE WHAT THE RELATIONSHIPS ARE AMONG THE FOLLOWING WORDS: SCALPEL IS TO SURGEON AS TRANSIT IS TO SURVEYOR (SCALPEL : SURGEON :: TRANSIT : SURVEYOR)

In this word analogy, *scalpel* refers to an instrument or a tool that a surgeon commonly uses for a specific purpose (cutting). *Surgeon* is an occupation. Logically then, a *transit* is most likely an instrument or a tool used in an occupation. Therefore, *surveyor* has to denote an occupation. Even if you do not know what a transit is (an instrument used to measure horizontal and vertical angles), you can deduce that the analogy is correct and that in this example the words are synonymous: instrument is to occupation as instrument is to occupation.

DISTINGUISHING BETWEEN THE CONNOTATIONS OF WORDS WITH SIMILAR DENOTATIONS

The connotation of a word is the unspoken meaning of the word beyond its dictionary meaning, or its denotation. It is the meaning that most people associate with that word; therefore it is a subjective interpretation of the meaning of the word, while a denotation is objective. For instance, the words "slender" and "skinny" both have a dictionary meaning of thin, but their connotations are quite different. "Slender" connotes thin as a stylish attribute, while "skinny" suggests an appearance that is undernourished, even unattractive. "Snake" is another example. The dictionary defines it as a reptile, but many people, when they hear the word "snake," associate it with someone who is not trustworthy.

DISCUSS THE DIFFERENCE IN THE CONNOTATIONS BETWEEN THE WORDS "WET" AND "DRENCHED."

"Wet" is a vague term; it could mean that you were caught in a rain drizzle or soaked to the bone. "Drenched," on the other hand, tells the reader that something is wet throughout. The connotations of "drenched" are much stronger than those of "wet." Drenched is an extreme condition, while wet is not. It is important to examine the context of the text where a word is to be used in order to choose an appropriate one. For instance, someone or something that is wet might be drenched, but it also might be moist or damp. Neither of these possibilities is remotely like drenched.

Improving Comprehension

It is important to acquire and use accurately words and phrases at the appropriate level so as to improve comprehension. This helps the student to excel in the classroom as well as on standardized testing. A student who has to stop continually while reading in order to look up the meaning of words or who doesn't understand the part of speech being used is unable to focus on the overall meaning of the text and will therefore be unable to draw conclusions. Use of the dictionary and thesaurus and other digital tools helps the student to determine meanings, especially the meanings of prefixes, suffixes, and root words.

English Language Arts/Literacy Practice Test #1

Practice Questions

Questions 1 – 5 are based on the following:

The Blue and the Gray

by Francis Miles Finch

By the flow of the inland river,
Whence the fleets of iron have fled,
Where the blades of the grave-grass quiver,
Asleep are the ranks of the dead:
Under the sod and the dew,
Waiting the judgment-day;
Under the one, the Blue,
Under the other, the Gray
These in the robings of glory,
Those in the gloom of defeat,
All with the battle-blood gory,
In the dusk of eternity meet:
Under the sod and the dew,
Waiting the judgment-day
Under the laurel, the Blue,
Under the willow, the Gray.
From the silence of sorrowful hours
The desolate mourners go,
Lovingly laden with flowers
Alike for the friend and the foe;
Under the sod and the dew,

Waiting the judgment-day;
Under the roses, the Blue,
Under the lilies, the Gray.

So with an equal splendor,
The morning sun-rays fall,
With a touch impartially tender,
On the blossoms blooming for all:
Under the sod and the dew,
Waiting the judgment-day;
Broidered with gold, the Blue,
Mellowed with gold, the Gray.

So, when the summer calleth,
On forest and field of grain,
With an equal murmur falleth
The cooling drip of the rain:
Under the sod and the dew,
Waiting the judgment-day,
Wet with the rain, the Blue
Wet with the rain, the Gray.

Sadly, but not with upbraiding,
The generous deed was done,
In the storm of the years that are fading
No braver battle was won:
Under the sod and the dew,
Waiting the judgment-day;
Under the blossoms, the Blue,
Under the garlands, the Gray

No more shall the war cry sever,

Or the winding rivers be red;

They banish our anger forever

When they laurel the graves of our dead!

Under the sod and the dew,

Waiting the judgment-day,

Love and tears for the Blue,

Tears and love for the Gray.

1. What type of scene does this poem depict?

a. the changing of the seasons
b. a loved one being welcomed home
c. the aftermath of a battle
d. a decision being made

2. What do the following lines imply about those who died as a result of the actions that were taken?

Love and tears for the Blue,
Tears and love for the Gray.

a. Those who died in battle are now weeping as a result of their destruction.
b. It doesn't matter who won the battle; there are people on both sides mourning their loved ones.
c. Bystanders are questioning the reasons for the battle that took so many lives.
d. One day, those who died will come back to life.

3. How does the author's repetition of the idea expressed in the following lines help communicate his main message?

Under the sod and the dew,

Waiting the judgment-day,

Love and tears for the Blue,

Tears and love for the Gray.

a. It shows that there are no winners when it comes to war, only destruction, and that in death, everyone is equal.
b. It tells the reader that battles should be remembered and reenacted to remember the losses once suffered.
c. It shows that those who die in battle should never be remembered for their sacrifices.
d. It reminds readers that it is not their job to wonder at the reasons behind war, but to follow the actions of others and mourn losses when they happen

4. To what war does this poem's title allude?

a. The Vietnam War
b. World War II
c. World War I
d. The Civil War

5. The author contrasts images of death and destruction with those of natural beauty and wonder to show that

a. war is pointless.
b. there are just reasons for war and violence.
c. even in the aftermath of horrific violence, life continues to go on and renew itself.
d. we should be thankful for what we have today and not worry about what we will need in the future.

Questions 6– 10 are based on the following:

The following is an excerpt from Anne of Green Gables, *a classic story written by Lucy Maud Montgomery that follows the life and times of a young girl who was mistakenly sent to live with an elderly brother and sister in rural Prince Edward Island.*

Morning at Green Gables

It was broad daylight when Anne awoke and sat up in bed, staring confusedly at the window through which a flood of cheery sunshine was pouring and outside of which something white and feathery waved across glimpses of blue sky.

For a moment she could not remember where she was. First came a delightful thrill, as something very pleasant; then a horrible remembrance. This was Green Gables and they didn't want her because she wasn't a boy!

But it was morning and, yes, it was a cherry-tree in full bloom outside of her window. With a bound she was out of bed and across the floor. She pushed up the sash—it went up stiffly and creakily, as if it hadn't been opened for a long time, which was the case; and it stuck so tight that nothing was needed to hold it up.

Anne dropped on her knees and gazed out into the June morning, her eyes glistening with delight. Oh, wasn't it beautiful? Wasn't it a lovely place? Suppose she wasn't really going to stay here! She would imagine she was. There was scope for imagination here.

A huge cherry-tree grew outside, so close that its boughs tapped against the house, and it was so thick-set with blossoms that hardly a leaf was to be seen. On both sides of the house were a big orchard, one of apple-trees and one of cherry-trees, also showered over with blossoms; and their grass was all sprinkled with dandelions. In the garden below were lilac-trees purple with flowers, and their dizzily sweet fragrance drifted up to the window on the morning wind.

Below the garden a green field lush with clover sloped down to the hollow where the brook ran and where scores of white birches grew, upspringing airily out of an undergrowth suggestive of delightful possibilities in ferns and mosses and woodsy things generally. Beyond it was a hill, green and feathery with spruce and fir; there was a gap in it where the gray gable end of the little house she had seen from the other side of the Lake of Shining Waters was visible.

Off to the left were the big barns and beyond them, away down over green, low-sloping fields, was a sparkling blue glimpse of sea.

Anne's beauty-loving eyes lingered on it all, taking everything greedily in. She had looked on so many unlovely places in her life, poor child; but this was as lovely as anything she had ever dreamed.

She knelt there, lost to everything but the loveliness around her, until she was startled by a hand on her shoulder. Marilla had come in unheard by the small dreamer.

"It's time you were dressed," she said curtly.

Marilla really did not know how to talk to the child, and her uncomfortable ignorance made her crisp and curt when she did not mean to be.

Anne stood up and drew a long breath.

"Oh, isn't it wonderful?" she said, waving her hand comprehensively at the good world outside.

"It's a big tree," said Marilla, "and it blooms great, but the fruit don't amount to much never—small and wormy."

"Oh, I don't mean just the tree; of course it's lovely—yes, it's RADIANTLY lovely—it blooms as if it meant it—but I meant everything, the garden and the orchard and the brook and the woods, the whole big dear world. Don't you feel as if you just loved the world on a morning like this? And I can hear the brook laughing all the way up here. Have you ever noticed what cheerful things brooks are? They're always laughing. Even in winter-time I've heard them under the ice. I'm so glad there's a brook near Green Gables. Perhaps you think it doesn't make any difference to me when you're not going to keep me, but it does. I shall always like to remember that there is a brook at Green Gables even if I never see it again. If there wasn't a brook I'd be HAUNTED by the uncomfortable feeling that there ought to be one. I'm not in the depths of despair this morning. I never can be in the morning. Isn't it a splendid thing that there are mornings? But I feel very sad. I've just been imagining that it was really me you wanted after all and that I was to stay here forever and ever. It was a great comfort while it lasted. But the worst of imagining things is that the time comes when you have to stop and that hurts."

"You'd better get dressed and come down-stairs and never mind your imaginings," said Marilla as soon as she could get a word in edgewise. "Breakfast is waiting. Wash your face and comb your hair. Leave the window up and turn your bedclothes back over the foot of the bed. Be as <u>smart</u> as you can."

This question has two parts. Answer part A, then answer part B.

6. Part A: Which words best describe how Anne is feeling?

a. shy and inactive
b. scared and unsure of her situation
c. energized and excited about the possibility that Green Gables will be her new home
d. excited, but a little homesick for the orphanage

Part B: Give a sentence from the passage that supports your answer in Part A.

____

____

This question has two parts. Answer part A, then answer part B.

7. Part A: The word <u>smart</u> as used in the final line of the passage means

a. quick
b. intelligent
c. painful
d. fashionable

Part B: Which word is the best synonym for <u>smart</u> based on your answer from Part A.

a. swift
b. tidy
c. fancy
d. intelligent

8. The narrator of this passage is

a. Anne
b. Marilla
c. an outside observer
d. an omniscient narrator who knows everything about the story and its characters

9. Which of the following describes how Marilla feels about Anne?

a. Marilla has decided that she does not like Anne, and will send her back to the orphanage.
b. Marilla is warming up to Anne and starting to feel affection for her.
c. Marilla is unsure of how to act around Anne, and is uncomfortable with a child in the house.
d. Marilla is suspicious of Anne and of whether her being sent to Green Gables was really a mistake.

10. What is the author's purpose in presenting the following as Anne's response to Marilla's misunderstanding of Anne gesturing out the window?

> "Oh, I don't mean just the tree; of course it's lovely—yes, it's RADIANTLY lovely—it blooms as if it meant it—but I meant everything, the garden and the orchard and the brook and the woods, the whole big dear world. Don't you feel as if you just loved the world on a morning like this? And I can hear the brook laughing all the way up here. Have you ever noticed what cheerful things brooks are? They're always laughing. Even in winter-time I've heard them under the ice. I'm so glad there's a brook near Green Gables. Perhaps you think it doesn't make any difference to me when you're not going to keep me, but it does. I shall always like to remember that there is a brook at Green Gables even if I never see it again. If there wasn't a brook I'd be HAUNTED by the uncomfortable feeling that there ought to be one. I'm not in the depths of despair this morning. I never can be in the morning. Isn't it a splendid thing that there are mornings? But I feel very sad. I've just been imagining that it was really me you wanted after all and that I was to stay here for ever and ever. It was a great comfort while it lasted. But the worst of imagining things is that the time comes when you have to stop and that hurts."

a. to show Anne's tendency for being dramatic and establish an important component of her personality
b. to show Anne's fear that Marilla misunderstood her intentions when she was gesturing out the window
c. to correct a misperception and prevent Marilla from being angry with Anne
d. to show Marilla the extent of Anne's intelligence in the hopes that she will not be sent back to the orphanage

Questions 11 – 15 are based on the following:

The following is an excerpt of an article published by The New York Times *announcing the assassination of President Abraham Lincoln.*

Awful Event

President Lincoln Shot by an Assassin

The Deed Done at Ford's Theatre Last Night

THE ACT OF A DESPERATE REBEL

The President Still Alive at Last Accounts

No Hopes Entertained of His Recovery

Attempted Assassination of Secretary Seward

DETAILS OF THE DREADFUL TRAGEDY.

Official

War Department, Washington April 15, 1:30 A.M. - Maj. Gen. Dis.: This evening at about 9:30 P.M. at Ford's Theatre, the President, while sitting in his private box with Mrs. Lincoln, Mr. Harris, and Major Rathburn, was shot by an assassin, who suddenly entered the box and appeared behind the President.

The assassin then leaped upon the stage, brandishing a large dagger or knife, and made his escape in the rear of the theatre.

The pistol ball entered the back of the President's head and penetrated nearly through the head. The wound is <u>mortal</u>. The President has been insensible ever since it was inflicted, and is now dying.

About the same hour an assassin, whether the same or not, entered Mr. Sewards' apartments, and under the pretense of having a prescription, was shown to the Secretary's sick chamber. The assassin immediately rushed to the bed, and inflicted two or three stabs on the throat and two on the face. It is hoped the wounds may not be mortal. My apprehension is that they will prove fatal.

The nurse alarmed Mr. Frederick Seward, who was in an adjoining room, and hastened to the door of his father's room, when he met the assassin, who inflicted upon him one or more dangerous wounds. The recovery of Frederick Seward is doubtful.

It is not probable that the President will live throughout the night.

Gen. Grant and wife were advertised to be at the theatre this evening, but he started to Burlington at 6 o'clock this evening.

At a Cabinet meeting at which Gen. Grant was present, the subject of the state of the country and the prospect of a speedy peace was discussed. The President was very cheerful and hopeful, and spoke very kindly of Gen. Lee and others of the Confederacy, and of the establishment of government in Virginia.

All the members of the Cabinet except Mr. Seward are now in attendance upon the President.

I have seen Mr. Seward, but he and Frederick were both unconscious.

Edwin M. Stanton, Secretary of War.

11. The underlined word <u>mortal</u> means:

a. recuperative.
b. painful.
c. fatal.
d. risky.

12. What is a likely purpose for including so many headlines at the start of the article?

a. to quickly convey the most important information about a significant event
b. to sensationalize a front-page news story
c. to incite panic in readers
d. to fill empty space on the page

13. Who is the author of this article?

a. The New York Times
b. Edwin M. Stanton
c. Frederick Seward
d. Major Rathburn

14. Write a summary of the article.

____

____

____

15. What is implied by the following sentence?

It is hoped the wounds may not be mortal. My apprehension is that they will prove fatal.

a. Those involved with the events are hopeful for a positive outcome.
b. There is no hope that Seward or Lincoln will recover from their wounds.
c. The writer is pessimistic about whether Seward will recover from his wounds.
d. The writer is doubtful about the legitimacy of accounts regarding the night's events.

Questions 16 – 20 are based on the following:

Carter's teacher asked him to write a short essay about whether or not everyone in America should vote. The following is the essay he wrote in response to this prompt from his seventh-grade social studies teacher.

(1) George Washington and all of the other great leaders who fought in the Revolutionary War would be very disappointed in Americans today. (2) The right to choose who will represent us in government has lost its importance. (3) Too many people do not vote in elections and are just throwing away their right our founding fathers fought to give them. (4) If people do not stand up and choose their own leaders, someone else will do it for them: and who knows what those leaders will stand for? (5) Many people struggled and died to give us the right to vote, and we should always honor that sacrifice by voting in every election.

(6) The main purpose of the Revolutionary War was to break free from rulers who did not give their people a say in their own government. (7) British colonists in America lived far away from their leaders in the British Parliament, and could not have a physical presence in government due to the distance between America and England. (8) This led to a denial of the rights that these colonists would have had if they still lived in England. (9) Tired of "taxation without representation," as the popular slogan went during this time in history, the colonists felt so strongly that they should have a say in their government that they took up arms against their own countrymen and fought for their freedom.

(10) Today, Americans take the fact that they have had voting rights for over 200 years for granted. (11) That's why voting isn't as important as it was back in the day. (12) If you look at how other people and countries have all fought for the right to vote, and continue to do so even today, it's plain to see that voting is something that should still be important in our society.

(13) We should all remember the sacrifices that have been made to ensure our freedoms, and we should take full advantage of those freedoms. (14) If we don't, those who died to ensure that all Americans have the right to life, liberty, and the pursuit of happiness will have died in vain. (15) I hope that my generation will be

the first of many to make voting one of our most important and treasured rights once again.

16. Which of the following answer choices presents the best revision of sentence 3?

a. Too many people do not vote in elections and just throw away their right our founding fathers fought to give them.
b. Too many people do not vote in elections, and, as a result, throw away one of the basic rights our founding fathers fought so hard to ensure for future generations.
c. Too many people today do not value their right to vote as much as our founding fathers.
d. Too many people choose not to vote in elections and throw away our founding fathers' rights.

17. Which of the following is the best way to revise sentence 11 so that the style the writer uses throughout the rest of the essay is maintained?

a. Our culture has devalued voting to the point that many simply do not care that an entire war was fought so that they could have that right in the first place.
b. Voting isn't as important as it was back in the day.
c. The devaluation of the right to vote by American society has resulted in the overall apathy of our citizenry when it comes to exercising the rights given to them as a result of the Revolutionary War.
d. People don't think of voting as important anymore.

18. Which sentence, if added after sentence 10, would make Carter's point in the third paragraph more persuasive?

a. The fights about voting rights that people in other countries are engaged in even now seem so far removed from life in the U.S.
b. Americans don't have any memory of having to fight for the right to have a voice in government.
c. For the most part, our citizens have had the right to vote for their entire lives; it's something that has just always been there.
d. They should remember that this right was something that had to be fought for, not something that was given to all citizens.

19. Which sentence states the main point of Carter's essay?

a. 2
b. 3
c. 4
d. 5

20. Which of the following pieces of advice would you give Carter to help him make his argument clearer and more persuasive?

a. Ask a few questions about why Americans today don't value their right to vote.
b. Provide more information about how and why Americans today do not value their right to vote, including examples and statistics.
c. Add in a personal story about your family's history as Revolutionary War activists.
d. Provide more information about why the British colonists chose to fight for independence.

Questions 21 – 23 are based on the following:

Jordan was asked to look at the following image showing the American/Mexican border and write about what she sees and how she feels about it. The following is her response to this image.

(1) This picture makes me feel conflicted. (2) The United States is shown on the left side; Mexico is on the right. (3) In the middle is a thin fence that separates two entire countries. (4) It seems insignificant in comparison to the great nations that lay on both sides of the fence. (5) But, like the fence itself, this line has been made by people to define what piece of land belongs to whom. (6) And hasn't this very thing been the cause of wars throughout history?

(7) You can see the huge difference between the two sides of the border. (8) The U.S. side is full of open land. (9) There are only a few buildings and maybe a small settlement, and there are also more walls. (10) It's like this area of land is a cushion between the dividing line and the U.S. (11) On the other side, you can see that the Mexican settlement is very developed. (12) A major highway travels the length of the border only a few yards away from the fence itself. (13) There are a lot of houses, businesses, signs, and other closely-packed signs of life and activity that seem to be pushed as close to the fence as possible.

(14) This interpretation of the image makes me sad. (15) It's like the country of Mexico is eager to have a more active partnership with its neighboring country, but America doesn't want any part of it. (16) The fact that the Mexican side gets as close to the dividing line as possible while the American side has a buffer area shows this. (17) It's like the two countries are sharing a sandbox, and America doesn't want Mexico's sand coming anywhere near its sand. (18) On the other hand, I also feel hopeful that one day both sides will be able to come together and play nice, sharing their sand and toys instead of building fences.

21. The purpose of sentence 11 is to

a. transition Jordan's discussion from details about the Mexican side of the border to details of the U.S. side of the border.
b. transition Jordan's discussion from details about the U.S. side of the border to details of the Mexican side of the border.
c. provide additional details to help the reader understand the content of the picture.
d. provide an opinion about what the purpose of the picture is.

This question has two parts. Answer part A, then answer part B.

22. Part A: Which sentence shows Jordan's opinion about the picture?

a. 12
b. 14
c. 15
d. 17

Part B: Based on your answer in Part A, which of the following sentences supports Jordan's opinion of the image?

a. 11
b. 13
c. 16
d. 17

23. Jordan's comparison of the relationship between the U.S. and Mexico to children playing in a sandbox is an example of using

a. a metaphor to better explain an abstract idea
b. a simile to draw a comparison between an abstract idea and a concrete detail
c. alliteration to emphasize a point
d. none of the above

24. Your teacher has asked you to write a research paper about global warming, and has asked you to come up with a research question first. Which of the following research questions would be most appropriate?

a. What year was the idea of global warming first presented to the world?
b. Who is the most recent scientist to conduct research on global warming?
c. What kind of impact does global warming have on our lives as Americans?
d. Who is the most outspoken advocate of efforts to combat global warming?

25. After you write a first draft of a language arts paper, what should you do next?

a. Turn it in for a grade.
b. Read through it and make changes as needed
c. Conduct research to learn about your topic
d. Draft an introduction.

26. The word "entreated" in the following sentence most nearly means what?

After being kidnapped and held for 10 days, Margaret entreated her captors to release her.

a. threw
b. sympathized
c. pleaded
d. angered

27. Which answer choice is the best correction for the following sentence?

Being the type of guy to hold a grudge after a bad breakup, there was no doubt that Max would refuse the invitation to his ex-girlfriend's wedding.

a. The invitation to his ex-girlfriend's wedding caused Max to remember that he was the type of guy who holds a grudge.
b. Max refused the invitation to his ex-girlfriend's wedding.
c. Being the type of guy to hold a grudge after a bad breakup, I didn't doubt that Max would refuse the invitation to his ex-girlfriend's wedding.
d. Being the type of guy to hold a grudge after a bad breakup, Max would refuse the invitation to his ex-girlfriend's wedding.

28. The proverb "A bird in the hand is better than two in the bush" means

a. you should always check the bushes when looking for birds.
b. you're better off counting on the things you have now, rather than on those you may or may not have in the future.
c. counting your opportunities is a good use of your time.
d. being afraid of the future is wasted energy.

29. Which of the following words is spelled correctly?

a. abbreviate
b. interum
c. imbellish
d. fulcurm

30. Which is the most effective way to rewrite the following sentence?

Preparing for the vocabulary test was a test of patience and a lot of hard work, but all my studying paid off in the end with my high score.

a. All of my studying paid off, even though studying for my vocabulary test was a test of my patience and a lot of hard work.
b. In the end, preparing for the vocabulary test was a test of patience and took a lot of hard work, but all my studying paid off in my score.
c. It took a lot of hard work and patience to study for my vocabulary test, but my high score made it all worth it in the end.
d. My high score on my vocabulary test proved that all of my studying and hard work were a test for me, but one that paid off.

31. If the word "antibacterial" describes a substance that kills bacteria, you can infer that the prefix "anti" means

a. original to.
b. against.
c. before.
d. under.

32. George is writing a paper and decides the sentence below should be rewritten.

Amelia suggested us eat it with ice cream and chocolate sauce.

Rewrite this sentence so that it is grammatically correct.

____

____

____

Use the paragraph below to answer questions 33 and 34.

I remember the day as if it were yesterday. It was Saturday afternoon and cloudless. The sun beat down upon my face, even through the chain link fenced dugout. It was so hot that I could feel my skin burning, and I was sweating, even though I wasn't on the field. I sat on the bench with a jug of water at my feet and a fistful of sunflower seeds. We were losing, three to one. I looked at our right fielder, Johnny, who was fanning his face with his glove as he was getting ready for the play.

33. What is the main idea of the paragraph?

a. Johnny is not a good baseball player.
b. This was a very hot Saturday afternoon.
c. The narrator was very thirsty while sitting on the bench.
d. The sunflower seeds were the only thing he had eaten all day.

34. Based on your answer in the previous question give two sentences that support the main idea.

____

____

____

____

Use the paragraph below to answer questions 35 and 36.

To celebrate their fifteenth wedding anniversary, my parents decided to take our family on vacation to London. This was the first time that I had ever been out of the country, and I was very excited. While in London, we discovered some really cool places, but my favorite was The Regent's Park in the City of Westminster in central London.

35. What is the purpose for the paragraph above?

a. To talk about the narrator's parents' anniversary
b. To introduce why the family was in London
c. To explain what it was like to travel to London
d. To explain why the narrator liked central London

36. What did the narrator most enjoy about the trip?

____

____

Questions 37 – 40 are based on the following:

Imagine a Better World

(1) My favorite song is "imagine" by John Lennon. (2) It was released in 1971. (3) It is one of the few famous songs that John Lennon recorded and sang alone. (4) For the majority of his career, John Lennon was a member of an iconic rock band called the Beatles, a band that changed the music industry. (5) The Beatles accepted a lot of success in their career, with popular songs such as "I Want to Hold Your Hand," "Come Together," "Let it Be," and "Here Comes the Sun." (6) After the band decided to separate, John Lennon became a solo artist as well as an promoter for peace.

(7) "Imagine" tells the story of Lennons dream of peace in the world. He asks the listener to imagine different situations. (8) He says to imagine that there are no countries, religions, or possessions. (9) He says, "I wonder if you can." (10) This line strikes me the most I try to imagine such a world. (11) When talking about no possessions, he continues and says, "No need for greed or hunger." (12) It is a great line. (13) Throughout the song, he says, "Imagine all the people." (14) And he gives examples. (15) At first he says, "living for today," and then moves on to say, "living life in peace," and finally, "sharing all the world."

(16) My favorite part of the song is the chorus. (17) Lennon says, "You may say I'm a dreamer, but I'm not the only one. (18) I hope someday you'll join us, and the world will be as one." (19) When I really listen to the words of this song, I realize that "Imagine" is so much more than something that sounds nicely. (20) Lennon is saying something very important and suggesting ways in which the world can live in peace. (21) Because of this song, I am a dreamer as well, and I join John Lennon in the fight for world peace.

37. What change, if any, should be made in sentence 1?

a. Change *favorite* to *favourite*
b. Change *imagine* to *Imagine*
c. Insert a comma after *song*
d. Make no change

38. What is the BEST verb to replace *accepted* in sentence 5?

a. Lasted
b. Liked
c. Had
d. Watched

39. What change should be made in sentence 6?

a. Change *separate* to *separated*
b. Insert a comma after *artist*
c. Change *solo* to *Solo*
d. Change *an* to *a*

40. What change, if any, should be made in sentence 7?

a. Change *Lennons* to *Lennon's*
b. Change *dream* to *dreamt*
c. Insert a comma after *peace*
d. Make no change

Answers and Explanations

1. C: There are many lines in this poem that indicate it is describing a scene following a battle: By the flow of the inland river / Whence the fleets of iron have fled; These in the robings of glory / Those in the gloom of defeat / All with the battle-blood gory / In the dusk of eternity meet; and No braver battle was won. Each of these lines implies that some kind of battle took place, but is now over.

2. B: These lines use the same words to describe the emotions of those on both sides of the conflict. The only difference is the order of the words, which does not affect their meaning in any way. This author is saying that there are tears and love for all of the people who lost their lives as a result of this battle. There is no indication that this is the view of the dead, or that, if indeed there are bystanders present in this section of the poem they are questioning anything. There is also no indication that the dead will come back to life.

3. A: These lines can be interpreted to mean that soldiers from both sides of the battle now lay dead and buried, and face the same fate. No matter the circumstances depicted in the lines preceding these in each stanza, the dead still lie beneath the soil awaiting the afterlife. This makes death an equalizer. The fact that this is repeated over and over in the poem shows its significance.

4. D: By describing the two conflicting factions in this battle as "The Blue" and "The Gray," the author alludes to the uniforms worn by Union and Confederate soldiers during the Civil War. There are no specific colors associated with any of the other wars listed.

5. C: The author begins the poem with images of ending and destruction, such as *in the gloom of defeat* and *All with the battle-blood gory / In the dusk of eternity meet*. Then, he transitions into a blending of these images with ones such as *the morning sun-rays fall* and *a touch impartially tender / On the blossoms blooming for all*. Since the images of nature begin to overshadow those of destruction as the poem progresses, it can be inferred that this is done purposefully to show that life goes on after war, that it has value, and that it is delicate.

6. Part A: C: There are plenty of small details throughout the passage that indicate that Anne is full of energy and excited about being at Green Gables, if a little fearful that her stay might only be temporary. The reader does not get a sense of fear or anxiety, except when Anne thinks about not being able to stay. Her statements and dramatic views of everything around her do not show Anne to be shy, inactive, or wanting to be back at the orphanage.

Part B: There are several sentences that can be used as examples but one good choice is, "She had looked on so many unlovely places in her life, poor child; but this was as lovely as anything she had ever dreamed."

7. Part A: A: Each of the answer choices is a possible definition of the word "smart," but answer A is the only one that fits the context in which it is used. In the passage, Marilla is showing a little impatience for Anne's long, fanciful descriptions of Green Gables, and is giving Anne instructions for what she needs to do before she goes down to breakfast. The reader can infer that Marilla doesn't want Anne to waste any time. Therefore, A is the best choice.

Part B: A: All of the answer choices are synonyms of smart but based on the way it is used in the story "swift" makes the most sense.

8. D: This story excerpt is told from the perspective of both Anne and Marilla, and the reader is privy to the thoughts of each. Only an all-knowing narrator would be able to know what both characters are thinking, and why.

9. C: Of all the answer choices, C makes the most sense, particularly in light of the following line: Marilla really did not know how to talk to the child, and her uncomfortable ignorance made her crisp and curt when she did not mean to be. The passage does not give the reader a sense that Marilla is suspicious or that she dislikes Anne, nor does it show her to be affectionate.

10. A: The fact that Anne's language in this section of the passage is very dramatic and reflects the romanticism of her earlier thoughts makes A the best choice here. There is no fear in the tone of this section, nor is there any indication that Anne is trying to prove herself.

11. C: Based on the sentence that follows the one in which "mortal" appears, it can be inferred that this word is describing the president's wound as fatal: *The wound is mortal. The President has been insensible ever since it was inflicted, and is now dying.*

12. A: This article has eight headlines, each containing more specific information than the one that comes before. Though some of the information presented in the headlines is clearly opinion, the overall message that is being communicated is informational: Lincoln was shot at Ford's theater; he's still alive, but not expected to survive. An attempt was also made on Secretary Seward's life.

13. B: The notation at the beginning of the article lets the reader know that the information provided is an official communication from the government. There is no author indicated at the beginning of the article. This is something that is included in most newspaper articles. However, the article is written in the first person, and the identity of the author is revealed at the end:

I HAVE SEEN MR. SEWARD, BUT HE AND FREDERICK WERE BOTH UNCONSCIOUS.
EDWIN M. STANTON, SECRETARY OF WAR.

Two of the answer choices reference people mentioned in the article. Finally, *The New York Times* is the publisher, not the author.

14. A good summary of the article would be something close to this:

President Lincoln was shot by an assassin at Ford's Theater; the president is not expected to survive. Secretary Seward and his son were also attacked by an assassin at their home this evening. They remain unconscious, and their chances of survival are questionable. General Grant was scheduled to be at the theater, but changed his plans and was not harmed by the evening's events.

15. C: The first sentence expresses hope that the wounds inflicted upon Seward are not so severe that he would not be able to recover. The second sentence expresses the writer's fear that this hope may be misplaced, and it conveys that he is anxious about Seward's fate.

16. B: This sentence is the most grammatically correct, and does not change the meaning of the original sentence. Answer A repeats the grammatical errors. Answers C and D change the meaning of the original sentence.

17. A: This revision mirrors the concise and more formal tone of the rest of the essay. Answers B and D are too short, and do not provide the context and explanation of the author's ideas like the other sentences in the essay do. Answer C is too formal and passive, whereas the rest of the essay has some conversational aspects to the language, and is, for the most part, active.

18. C: This sentence directly supports the idea in the previous sentence about people taking their voting rights for granted. It shows that people don't have personal experience with being denied this right, and sets up the next sentence. Answers A and D do not make sense in the context of the discussion in this paragraph. Answer B does not support sentence 10 or lead into sentence 11 as effectively as answer C.

19. D: This sentence sums up Carter's position and reason for writing the essay. He is clearly arguing that people should take the right to vote more seriously than they do today, which is what this sentence says. The sentences that lead up to it provide context for this point.

20. B: Carter's essay talks a lot about people and attitudes during the Revolutionary War, but not much about how and why Americans today do not value their right to vote. Discussing this side of his argument will balance out his logic and make his essay more persuasive.

21. B: The three sentences preceding sentence 11 talk about what is on the U.S. side of the border. The sentences that follow talk about what is on the Mexican side. Sentence 11 transitions the discussion from one set of details to the other.

22. Part A: D: Answers A and B address ideas in the paragraph before Jordan's interpretation is mentioned, and don't apply here. Answer C provides a supporting detail, but answer D really shows why Jordan sees this image as sad.

Part B: C: This sentence explains why she feels sad. She explains Mexico gets as close to America as possible while America looks like they don't want to have anything to do with Mexico.

23. A: Comparing a complex relationship, such as the one between countries, to something less complex and seemingly unrelated, such as children playing, is an example of metaphor. Similes use "like" or "as" to compare two things. Alliteration uses similar starting sounds to create a specific effect.

24. C: Research questions are ones that have complex answers that can act as the thesis of an essay. This is the only question that has an answer that is not a specific person or date, which are simple answers.

25. B: After you complete a first draft, you need to revise it for content and structure. Turning it in for a grade should happen after you have completed all of the steps of the writing process. You should conduct research on your topic before you begin writing. An introduction should be included as part of the first draft.

26. C: The sentence is about a woman who has been held against her will for many days. It makes sense that she would plead or beg for her release. That she would throw, sympathize, or anger for her release does not.

27. D: Answer D is the best choice, as it corrects the misplaced modifier error in the sentence. Max is clearly the subject of the sentence, and therefore his name needs to be the first word after the comma. Answers A and B change the meaning of the sentence. Answer C repeats the same error as the one found in the original sentence.

28. B: This proverb talks about something that you can hold, see, and feel now being better than something that *could* be somewhere else. Answer B is the only choice that provides this type of comparison. It also makes the most logical sense.

29. A: Answer B should be "interim," answer C should be "embellish," and answer D should be "fulcrum."

30. C: This answer choice is the simplest and most efficient way of expressing the same ideas that are in the original sentence. The remainder of the answer choices contain redundancies, passive language, and poor sentence structure.

31. B: If something that is antibacterial kills bacteria, it can't be original to it, before it, or under it. The antibacterial agent goes against what enables the bacteria to live.

32. The correct way to write this sentence is:

"Amelia suggested that we eat it with ice cream and chocolate sauce."

33. B: All of the other choices were mentioned in the paragraph, but they were not the main idea. He talks about the sun "beating down", and then talks about Johnny fanning himself top stay cool.

34. Both of the sentences below support the fact that it is very hot outside.

"The sun beat down upon my face, even through the chain link fenced dugout." "I looked at our right fielder, Johnny, who was fanning his face with his glove as he was getting ready for the play."

35. C: In this paragraph the narrator is telling about what it is like to travel to London.

36. In the paragraph he states that his "favorite was The Regent's Park in the City of Westminster"

37. B: because *imagine* is a proper noun. As the title of a song, it requires capitalization. A is not correct. *Favorite* is spelled correctly. C is not correct. *My favorite song* is not an introductory clause, so a comma is not needed.

38. C: The missing verb in this sentence must have something to do with possession since it discusses the band's success. *Had* indicates possession. A, B, and D are incorrect, because these verbs do not fit within the sentence.

39. D: It is correct because in the sentence, the article *an* is followed by a noun, *promoter. Promoter* begins with a consonant and a consonant sound and therefore must be followed by the article *a.* A is not correct. The verb in this sentence is *decided*, not *separate*, and therefore *separate* does not need to be in the past tense like the rest of the paragraph. B is not correct because the comma is unnecessary. C is not correct. *Solo* is not a proper noun and does not need to be capitalized.

40. A: because *Lennon* is possessive in this sentence; therefore, it requires an apostrophe. B is not correct. In this sentence, *dream* is a noun rather than a verb, so it does not need to be in the past tense. C is not correct, because a comma is unnecessary.

English Language Arts/Literacy Practice Test #2

Practice Questions

Questions 1 – 4are based on the following:

The following is an excerpt from The House of Mirth *by Edith Wharton. This novel tells the tragic tale of Lily Bart, a beautiful woman who lives the life of a socialite, even though she herself has no money, and must marry in order to maintain the lifestyle to which she has become accustomed. To do this, she must maintain her reputation as a desirable catch for wealthy suitors.*

In the hansom she leaned back with a sigh. Why must a girl pay so dearly for her least escape from routine? Why could one never do a natural thing without having to screen it behind a structure of artifice? She had yielded to a passing impulse in going to Lawrence Selden's rooms, and it was so seldom that she could allow herself the luxury of an impulse! This one, at any rate, was going to cost her rather more than she could afford. She was vexed to see that, in spite of so many years of vigilance, she had blundered twice within five minutes. That stupid story about her dress-maker was bad enough—it would have been so simple to tell Rosedale that she had been taking tea with Selden! The mere statement of the fact would have rendered it innocuous. But, after having let herself be surprised in a falsehood, it was doubly stupid to snub the witness of her discomfiture. If she had had the presence of mind to let Rosedale drive her to the station, the concession might have purchased his silence. He had his race's accuracy in the appraisal of values, and to be seen walking down the platform at the crowded afternoon hour in the company of Miss Lily Bart would have been money in his pocket, as he might himself have phrased it. He knew, of course, that there would be a large house-party at Bellomont, and the possibility of being taken for one of Mrs. Trenor's guests was doubtless included in his calculations. Mr. Rosedale was still at a stage in his social ascent when it was of importance to produce such impressions.

The provoking part was that Lily knew all this—knew how easy it would have been to silence him on the spot, and how difficult it might be to do so afterward. Mr. Simon Rosedale was a man who made it his business to know everything about every one, whose idea of showing himself to be at home in society was to display an inconvenient familiarity with the habits of those with whom he wished to be thought intimate. Lily was sure that within twenty-four hours the story of her visiting her dress-maker at the Benedick would be in active circulation among Mr. Rosedale's acquaintances. The worst of it was that she had always snubbed and ignored him. On his first appearance—when her improvident cousin, Jack Stepney, had obtained for him (in return for favours too easily guessed) a card to one of the vast impersonal Van Osburgh "crushes"—Rosedale, with that mixture of artistic sensibility and business astuteness which characterizes his race, had instantly gravitated toward Miss Bart. She understood his motives, for her own course was guided by as nice calculations. Training and experience had taught her to be hospitable to newcomers, since the most unpromising might be useful later on, and there were plenty of available oubliettes to swallow them if they were not. But some intuitive repugnance, getting the better of years of social discipline, had made her push Mr. Rosedale into his oubliette without a trial. He had left behind only the ripple of amusement which his speedy dispatch had caused among her friends; and though later (to shift the metaphor) he reappeared lower down the stream, it was only in fleeting glimpses, with long submergences between.

Hitherto Lily had been undisturbed by scruples. In her little set Mr. Rosedale had been pronounced "impossible," and Jack Stepney roundly snubbed for his attempt to pay his debts in dinner invitations. Even Mrs. Trenor, whose taste for variety had led her into some hazardous experiments, resisted Jack's attempts to disguise Mr. Rosedale as a novelty, and declared that he was the same little Jew who had been served up and rejected at the social board a dozen times within her memory; and while Judy Trenor was obdurate there was small chance of Mr. Rosedale's penetrating beyond the outer limbo of the Van Osburgh crushes. Jack gave up the contest with a laughing "You'll see," and, sticking manfully to his guns, showed himself with Rosedale at the fashionable restaurants, in company with the personally vivid if socially obscure ladies who are available for such purposes. But the attempt had hitherto been vain, and as Rosedale undoubtedly paid for the dinners, the laugh remained with his debtor.

Mr. Rosedale, it will be seen, was thus far not a factor to be feared—unless one put one's self in his power. And this was precisely what Miss Bart had done. Her clumsy fib had let him see that she had something to conceal; and she was sure he had a score to settle with her. Something in his smile told her he had not forgotten. She turned from the thought with a little shiver, but it hung on her all the way to the station, and dogged her down the platform with the persistency of Mr. Rosedale himself.

1. This passage is told from whose point of view?

a. Simon Rosedale
b. Lily Bart
c. Jack Stepney
d. Lawrence Selden

2. In the film version of *The House of Mirth*, this scene is portrayed by three actors. The audience observes Lily, Selden, and Rosedale meeting outside the Benedick, and watches the events that unfold. This change of medium makes analyzing the events through Lily's thoughts impossible, so much of the back story presented in the text is lost in the film version. What detail would most likely be missed by telling the story through the medium of film?

a. Lily does not like Rosedale, but will keep up the pretenses of being sociable and polite to him in public.
b. Lily is uncomfortable with the situation she is in.
c. Lily lied about her reason for being at the Benedick.
d. Rosedale has ulterior motives for offering Lily a ride.

3. What does "sticking manfully to his guns" mean as it is used in this passage?

a. Jack Stepney could easily turn violent in the face of society's rejection of Rosedale.
b. Rosedale is continuing to persist in his efforts to break into Lily's circle of friends, but is becoming discouraged by their constant rejection of him.
c. Rosedale is optimistic that if he persists in his efforts to break into Lily's circle of friends, he will eventually be successful.
d. Jack Stepney is standing behind his public support of Rosedale in important social circles, despite the fact that important members of society have snubbed them both for it.

4. References to Rosedale's "race" and lines such as "that he was the same little Jew who had been served up and rejected at the social board a dozen times within her memory" reveal what about Lily's set of friends?

a. They are envious of Rosedale's success and charisma.
b. They are afraid of Rosedale because of his family lineage.
c. They are discriminating against Rosedale because he is Jewish.
d. They are mistaken about where Rosedale's wealth came from.

Questions 5 – 8 are based on the following:

"The Gettysburg Address" was a speech given by President Abraham Lincoln on Nov. 19, 1863 at the dedication of the Gettysburg National Cemetery, the final resting place of soldiers killed in the Battle of Gettysburg during the Civil War.

The Gettysburg Address

Four score and seven years ago our fathers brought forth, upon this continent, a new nation, conceived in Liberty, and dedicated to the proposition that all men are created equal.

Now we are engaged in a great civil war, testing whether that nation, or any nation so conceived, and so dedicated, can long endure. We are met here on a great battlefield of that war. We have come to dedicate a portion of it as a final resting place for those who here gave their lives that that nation might live. It is altogether fitting and proper that we should do this.

But in a larger sense we cannot dedicate - we cannot consecrate - we cannot hallow this ground. The brave men, living and dead, who struggled here, have consecrated it far above our poor power to add or detract. The world will little note, nor long remember, what we say here, but can never forget what they did here.

It is for us, the living, rather to be dedicated here to the unfinished work which they have, thus far, so nobly carried on. It is rather for us to be here dedicated to the great task remaining before us - that from these honored dead we take increased devotion to that cause for which they here gave the last full measure of devotion - that we here highly resolve that these dead shall not have died in vain; that this nation shall have a new birth of freedom; and that this government of the people, by the people, for the people, shall not perish from the earth.

5. What is the main message of this speech?

a. Those who died in this battle honor this land we are dedicating today better than anyone else.
b. As we honor those who died in this battle, we should move forward with renewed dedication to ensuring the nation our founding fathers created continues to function the way they intended.
c. We need to put the regrets of the past aside, without remembering the sacrifices of those who gave their lives for our country.
d. The war we are fighting is far from over, as evidenced by the number of lives lost in this battle.

6. The phrase "the world will little note" means what?

a. The world will not soon forget.
b. The world will record what we say here.
c. The world will not pay much attention.
d. The world will recall what we do with perfect accuracy.

7. Why does Lincoln most likely talk about the past before he talks about the present?

a. to incite listeners of his message to protest
b. to remember what has been lost in the past
c. to establish context for his main message
d. to try to get listeners to side with his position

8. What is the following sentence addressing?

Now we are engaged in a great civil war, testing whether that nation, or any nation so conceived, and so dedicated, can long endure.

a. whether or not a nation based on ideas of freedom and equality can survive for any significant length of time
b. whether or not the Union will be able to preserve the existing structure of the United States by preventing the Confederacy from seceding
c. whether or not the Confederacy will be successful in seceding from the United States and surviving on its own
d. whether or not Lincoln should continue dedicating troops to the war

Questions 9 – 13 are based on the following:

Joey wanted to learn more about the U.S. Coast Guard, and chose it as his topic when his teacher asked each student to write an informational essay. A draft of his essay follows.

(1) The United States Coast Guard was founded in 1790 as the branch of military service responsible for safeguarding the country's sea-related interests. (2) It was originally created to protect the U.S. from smugglers, and to enforce tariff and trade laws. (3) It may seem like this would be a job for the Navy, but the purpose of the Navy is very different from that of the Coast Guard. (4) The Navy's job is to engage in combat and defend the seas from threats to the U.S. and its interests worldwide. (5) The Coast Guard is actually a part of the Department of Homeland Security, and is considered a federal law enforcement agency. (6) Its mission is to protect and enforce laws on our coastlines and in our ports, and to safeguard other interests within American waters.

(7) In addition to its role as a maritime law enforcement agency, the Coast Guard also serves as a guardian of the environment. (8) This includes stopping waste and other types of pollution from being dumped into the ocean, preventing and helping to clean up oil spills, and even ensuring that species of marine life that could threaten the balance of existing environments are prevented from being introduced. (9) This is a very important job for the Coast Guard, because there would not be much of a coastline to protect if our seas were too polluted to enjoy and sustain us.

(10) On the whole, Coast Guard personnel perform the following in a single day: save 12 lives; respond to 64 search and rescue cases; keep 842 pounds of cocaine off the streets; service 116 buoys and fix 24 discrepancies; screen 720 commercial vessels, and 183,000 crew and passengers; issue 173 credentials to merchant mariners; investigate 13 marine accidents; inspect 68 containers and 29 vessels for compliance with air emissions standards; perform 28 safety and environmental examinations of foreign vessels; board 13 fishing boats to ensure compliance with fisheries laws; and respond and investigate 10 pollution incidents.

(11) In addition to the day-to-day role of the Coast Guard, this branch of service also plays an important role in many large-scale and humanitarian operations. (12) In 2010, the Coast Guard launched a mission to provide assistance directly following the devastating earthquake in Haiti. (13) It was there in response to the *Deepwater Horizon* explosion that caused the dumping of millions of gallons of crude oil in to the Gulf of Mexico. (14) It was there to seize $80 million worth of cocaine out of the hands of smugglers.

9. Which paragraph establishes the subject and context of this article?

a. paragraph 1
b. paragraph 2
c. paragraph 3
d. paragraph 4

10. Write a sentence that if placed before sentence 10, would create a better transition from the second paragraph to the third paragraph.

____

____

____

11. Adding which of the following sentences to paragraph 3 would make it more credible?

a. This information comes from the official Coast Guard Web site.
b. The average age of Coast Guard members is 28.
c. The Coast Guard has a long history of service.
d. There are 33,200 enlisted Coast Guard members.

12. Which of the following would be the best conclusion for this essay?

a. There is much more that we can learn about the Coast Guard. To list all of the great things about this organization would take all day. The opportunities available to members of the Coast Guard are endless, and we should all consider becoming a "Coastie."
b. Being a "Coastie" would be the fulfillment of anyone's dreams. Who wouldn't want a career that is full of adventure and honor? There is no better job that a person could pursue as their life's work.
c. The Coast Guard is a very diverse and exciting branch of the U.S. military. Though many may not believe it is as important as the Navy, the Army, the Marines, or the Air Force, it's plain to see that the Coast Guard plays a vital role in ensuring our nation's security and prosperity.
d. The Coast Guard provides little support toward defending our nation from threats, as its members are always so close to home. Greater purpose can be found in a different branch of service. The threats that the Coast Guard faces are insignificant when compared to those faced by the Army, the Navy, the Marines, or the Air Force.

13. Joey's teacher likes his essay, but wants him to revise it so that it focuses more on the role of the Coast Guard in U.S. history. Which of the following would be the best place for him to look to find out what the Coast Guard did to protect our shores during World War II?

a. *The* Greatest Battles of WWII documentary from the History Channel
b. An article entitled "U.S. Coast Guard Combat Victories of World War II" on the official Coast Guard Web site
c. An entry entitled "World War II" found in the Encyclopedia Britannica
d. An article entitled "History of the United States Navy" found on Wikipedia

Questions 14 – 17 are based on the following:

Brett was asked to write a short narrative about his most memorable experience. A draft of his essay follows.

(1) My most memorable experience was meeting my baby sister for the first time. (2) Though I knew that my mom was pregnant, I don't think I was really aware of what that meant and how it would change my life until I saw Megan's little face for the very first time.

(3) I loved my mom and dad. (4) I loved my life. (5) I loved being the center of their attention. (6) Playing with Mom and Dad was the best. (7) As my mom began to get bigger, though, she couldn't play with me as much. (8) I couldn't understand why she was so tired all of the time, or why she couldn't run around with me at the soccer field like she used to. (9) My dad said that it was because of the new baby that was inside of her. (10) That was when I started to hate the baby.

(11) Who was she to take so much energy from my mom and prevent her from playing with me? (12) Why were my parents so concerned about this kid that wasn't even here yet, and what would happen when she got here? (13) Did all of this mean that I would always get the short end of the stick?

(14) I started to worry that once the baby came, my parents would forget all about me. (15) The baby would be the only thing they thought about, the only thing they cared about. (16) I would get lost in the shuffle because I wasn't their only child anymore.

(17) You can imagine how upset I was the day my mom went into labor, and my parents sent me to stay with my grandma until the baby was born. (18) Everything I'd been fearing and stressing about for months was about to come true. (19) Thinking back, I'm really embarrassed that I threw a tantrum and added to my parents' difficulties that day. (20) I was scared, though. (21) I thought I was losing the two most important people in my life.

(22) I didn't want to go to the hospital to see my new baby sister, but my grandma made me go. (23) I'm so glad she did. (24) When we got to my mom's room, my dad came out and gave me the biggest hug I'd ever gotten.

(25) "Hey, big brother," he said. (26) "Ready to meet the person who is going to think you are the coolest person in the world?"

(27) When I saw my mom, she handed the baby to my dad and held out her arms to me. (28) I crawled onto her bed and hugged her as hard as I could. (29) Though I knew she was in pain from her C-section, she still stroked my hair and whispered "I love you, baby" in my ear. (30) She made a place for me on her lap, and then cradled the baby so that I could see her little face for the first time.

(31) "Megan, meet the best big brother that anyone could ask for," my mom said to the baby.

(32) I knew then that nothing would come between my parents and me. (33) They could pour all of their love into me and still have enough love for my little sister. (34) And I learned that I had enough love in me for a new member of our family, too. (35) As Baby Megan slept quietly in my mom's arms, her little hand grabbed onto my finger and squeezed it tight, like I was the only safe thing in the world she could grasp.

14. What do the questions in paragraph 3 tell the reader about Brett's experience?

a. He was angry, confused, and resentful toward his mother's pregnancy and his little sister.
b. He was undecided about how he felt about his mother's pregnancy.
c. He was excited about the prospect of becoming a big brother for the first time.
d. He was both happy and upset about the prospect of becoming a big brother for the first time.

This question has two parts. Answer Part A then Part B.

15. Part A: Which sentence in paragraph 5 gives the best description of how Brett is feeling?

a. sentence 18
b. sentence 19
c. sentence 20
d. sentence 21

Part B: Which sentence could be deleted from paragraph 5 without changing the overall message of the paragraph?

a. sentence 17
b. sentence 19
c. sentence 20
d. sentence 21

16. Which of the following sentences from the essay most clearly explains why the birth of Brett's sister was his most memorable experience?

a. I knew then that nothing would come between my parents and me.
b. When we got to my mom's room, my dad came out and gave me the biggest hug I'd ever gotten.
c. And I learned that I had enough love in me for a new member of our family, too.
d. None of the above; Brett doesn't explain in his essay why the birth of his sister was his most memorable experience.

17. Which of the following sentences would be the best conclusion for this essay?

a. The love that I felt in that moment overwhelmed me, making it an experience I will remember all of my life.
b. There was nothing in the world that could have stopped me from becoming the best big brother I could be.
c. My parents' love had given me the strength to make it through this moment, and I will be forever grateful for their support.
d. Though I was willing to accept that I was no longer an only child, I also knew that from this moment on, nothing would ever really be the same.

Questions 18 – 20 are based on the following:

The following address was given by President Franklin D. Roosevelt on Dec. 8, 1941, the day after Pearl Harbor was attacked by Japan.

> Mr. Vice President, Mr. Speaker, Members of the Senate, and of the House of Representatives:
>
> Yesterday, December 7th, 1941 -- a date which will live in infamy -- the United States of America was suddenly and deliberately attacked by naval and air forces of the Empire of Japan.
>
> The United States was at peace with that nation and, at the solicitation of Japan, was still in conversation with its government and its emperor looking toward the maintenance of peace in the Pacific.
>
> Indeed, one hour after Japanese air squadrons had commenced bombing in the American island of Oahu, the Japanese ambassador to the United States and his colleague delivered to our Secretary of State a formal reply to a recent American message. And while this reply stated that it seemed useless to continue the existing diplomatic negotiations, it contained no threat or hint of war or of armed attack.
>
> It will be recorded that the distance of Hawaii from Japan makes it obvious that the attack was deliberately planned many days or even weeks ago. During the intervening time, the Japanese government has deliberately sought to deceive the United States by false statements and expressions of hope for continued peace.
>
> The attack yesterday on the Hawaiian islands has caused severe damage to American naval and military forces. I regret to tell you that very many American lives have been lost. In addition, American ships have been reported torpedoed on the high seas between San Francisco and Honolulu.
>
> Yesterday, the Japanese government also launched an attack against Malaya.

Last night, Japanese forces attacked Hong Kong.

Last night, Japanese forces attacked Guam.

Last night, Japanese forces attacked the Philippine Islands.

Last night, the Japanese attacked Wake Island.

And this morning, the Japanese attacked Midway Island.

Japan has, therefore, undertaken a surprise offensive extending throughout the Pacific area. The facts of yesterday and today speak for themselves. The people of the United States have already formed their opinions and well understand the implications to the very life and safety of our nation.

As commander in chief of the Army and Navy, I have directed that all measures be taken for our defense. But always will our whole nation remember the character of the onslaught against us.

No matter how long it may take us to overcome this premeditated invasion, the American people in their righteous might will win through to absolute victory.

I believe that I interpret the will of the Congress and of the people when I assert that we will not only defend ourselves to the uttermost, but will make it very certain that this form of treachery shall never again endanger us.

Hostilities exist. There is no blinking at the fact that our people, our territory, and our interests are in grave danger.

With confidence in our armed forces, with the unbounding determination of our people, we will gain the inevitable triumph -- so help us God.

I ask that the Congress declare that since the unprovoked and dastardly attack by Japan on Sunday, December 7th, 1941, a state of war has existed between the United States and the Japanese empire.

This question has two parts. Answer Part A then Part B.

18. Part A: Which of the following is a fact presented in this address?

a. No matter how long it may take us to overcome this premeditated invasion, the American people in their righteous might will win through to absolute victory.
b. But always will our whole nation remember the character of the onslaught against us.
c. I believe that I interpret the will of the Congress and of the people when I assert that we will not only defend ourselves to the uttermost, but will make it very certain that this form of treachery shall never again endanger us.
d. Last night, Japanese forces attacked Hong Kong.

Part B: Give a sentence from the address that is an opinion.

____

____

____

19. Where might you look to find more information about the bombing of Pearl Harbor?

a. an American history textbook
b. home movies
c. transcripts of interviews with the mayor of your town
d. transcripts of interviews with the current president

20. Based on the information presented, you think that Congress should approve the president's request to declare war. What reasoning might you use to convince your class you are right?

a. Roosevelt is the president, and his authority should not be questioned.
b. Roosevelt's reasoning is heartfelt and it feels like the right thing to do, even if there are not enough facts presented.
c. The president presents a compelling case supported by facts and logic that makes sense.
d. Roosevelt is clearly considering the consequences such a decision would have on his political party.

Use the following image to answer questions 21 – 23.

21. What is most likely happening in the picture?

a. People have gathered at a cemetery for some kind of memorial service.
b. A little boy is visiting the grave of a loved one.
c. A celebration for a national holiday is being held.
d. There is no way to tell what is happening in the picture.

22. How would you describe the mood of the scene?

a. jovial and celebratory
b. solemn and reverent
c. bright and airy
d. severe and admonitory

23. What is the likely purpose of the photo?

a. to show the ideology behind a historic event
b. to make a political statement about a recent event
c. to show the lasting impact of a tragic event
d. to inform the public about a recent event

This question has two parts. Answer Part A then Part B.

24. Part A: What is the grammatical error in the following sentence?

Aware that his decision would affect the rest of his life, the college Ben chose was Harvard.

a. The subject and the verb do not agree.
b. The sentence contains a comma splice.
c. There is a dangling modifier.
d. There is no error.

Part B: Based on your answer in Part A, rewrite the sentence below.

____

____

____

25. Which word in the following sentence is an adverb?

The present was wrapped expertly by a professional at the store.

a. present
b. wrapped
c. expertly
d. professional

26. What does the underlined word in the following sentence mean?

The students' excitement about the beginning of summer vacation <u>pervaded</u> the whole classroom.

a. stood at attention
b. spread throughout
c. explained
d. took note

27. The phrase "going into the fold" refers to

a. joining or rejoining a group.
b. rejecting an idea.
c. holding true to a belief.
d. starting a new journey.

28. hyperventilation : air :: hyperthermia :

a. hair
b. air
c. heat
d. money

29. Which sentence is punctuated correctly?

a. We were uncertain about the terrain ahead; and had lost the map.
b. These were the items on the shopping list: eggs, milk, bread, peanut butter, and jelly.
c. Is there any way that we can meet later.
d. Mary had an appointment at 3 p.m.; George had one at 4 p.m.

30. Which of the following answer choices is spelled correctly?

a. intrude
b. aclimate
c. wisen
d. alude

31. Where would you look if you needed to find another word for "pardon"?

a. a dictionary
b. a thesaurus
c. an index
d. a glossary

Questions 32 – 38 pertain to the following passage:

The Educational Market Town

(1) Aberystwyth is a market town on the West Coast of Wales within the United Kingdom. A market town refers to European areas that have the right to have markets, which differentiates it from a city or village. The town is located where two rivers meet, the River Ystwyth and River Rheidol and is the best known as an educational center, housing an established university since 1872.

(2) The town is situated between North Wales and South Wales, and is a large vacation destination as well as tourist attraction. Constitution Hill is a hill on the north end of Aberystwyth, which provides excellent views of Cardigan Bay and which is supported by the Aberystwyth Electric Cliff Railway. Although Aberystwyth is known as a modern Welsh town, it is home to several historic buildings, such as the remnants of a castle.

(3) Although there are several grocery, clothing, sporting goods, and various other miscellaneous shops, Aberystwyth is best known for its educational services. Aberystwyth University, formerly known as University College Wales, as well as the National Library of Wales, which is the legal deposit library for Wales and which houses all Welsh publications, are both located within Aberystwyth. The two main languages traditionally spoken in Aberystwyth are English and Welsh. With local live music, arts center, and educational opportunities in gorgeous scenery, Aberystwyth is a hidden luxury within the United Kingdom.

32. Where is Aberystwyth located?

a. England
b. Ireland
c. Scotland
d. Wales

33. What is the purpose of this essay?

a. To explain that the university was established in 1872
b. To explain the legal deposit library in Wales
c. To provide a portrait of a town
d. To explain the views in Aberystwyth

34. What does the word situated mean in paragraph 2?

a. located
b. fighting
c. luxurious
d. hidden

35. Which of the following statements is an opinion?

a. Although Aberystwyth is known as a modern Welsh town, it is home to several historic buildings, such as the remnants of a castle
b. With local live music, arts center, and educational opportunities in gorgeous scenery, Aberystwyth is a hidden luxury within the United Kingdom
c. The two main languages traditionally spoken in Aberystwyth are English and Welsh
d. Aberystwyth is a market town on the West Coast of Wales within the United Kingdom

36. How many languages are traditionally spoken in Aberystwyth?

a. One
b. Two
c. Three
d. More than three

37. What makes Aberystwyth a market town?

a. It is a city
b. It is a village
c. It has the right to have a market
d. There are markets in town every day

38. What is Constitution Hill supported by?

a. Cardigan Bay
b. The Ocean
c. North Wales
d. Aberystwyth Electric Cliff Railway

Answer questions 39 and 40 based on the chart below.

Betty's Boutique Sales Report (sales amounts in thousands of dollars)					
Department	**1 Qtr 2008**	**2 Qtr 2008**	**3 Qtr 2008**	**4 Qtr 2008**	**1 Qtr 2009**
Women's wear	157	153	153	149	157
Men's wear	96	90	87	86	88
Children	63	55	56	54	57
Accessories	85	81	76	73	73
Shoes	70	68	68	67	68
Hair and Body	66	59	60	57	61

39. Which department's sales decreased by the biggest percentage from first quarter 2008 to first quarter 2009?

a. Women's wear
b. Accesories
c. Shoes
d. Hair and Body

40. During which quarter were overall store sales the lowest?

a. 1st quarter 2008
b. 2nd quarter 2008
c. 3rd quarter 2008
d. 4th quarter 2008

Answers and Explanations

1. B: All of the details that are given about people and events are presented from Lily's point of view. They are not objective, and reflect her reactions and opinions.

2. D: This detail comes from Lily's internal dialogue. The reader is privy to this since the story is told from her perspective. Everything is filtered through her perspective and knowledge. As a viewer of a film portrayal, this perspective is completely changed from that of a participant to that of an observer. The scene could plainly depict the details in answers A through C, but the detail in answer D is part of Lily's internal analysis, which would not be part of a film scene.

3. D: This part of the passage talks about how Jack Stepney keeps bringing Rosedale to fashionable places and events, and how he is snubbed for his actions. Rosedale is snubbed, too. Yet, he persists, saying "You'll see" to the naysayers. The answers that focus on Rosedale are incorrect, and there is no discussion of violence, as "sticking to one's guns" is used figuratively here.

4. C: The places where Rosedale's race is referenced and the line cited in this question allude to anti-Semitic attitudes toward the man.

5. B: Lincoln begins this speech by discussing the founding of our country and what the original purpose of the U.S. was. Then, he goes on to talk about how the U.S is currently engaged in a war intended to fracture the nation, and he states that the battle being discussed was one large tragedy that came out of the war. Next, Lincoln says that his speech and even the memorial itself can't truly honor those who died, and that it's up to those who survived to continue the fight to ensure the nation does not break apart. Answer B best communicates this message.

6. C: The sentence in which this phrase is found is: The world will little note, nor long remember, what we say here, but can never forget what they did here. In this context, the phrase "the world will little note" means that no one outside of those in attendance or possibly those outside the country will pay attention to the speech or the ceremony. This eliminates all of the answer choices except C.

7. C: There is a comparison between the ideas of the Revolution and the Civil War in this speech. To facilitate understanding of this comparison, Lincoln has to set the stage by telling his audience about the past event he is referencing. This establishes the context of his message.

8. A: This line directly references the idea in the previous paragraph, which is that the U.S. is a nation that was created to ensure liberty and equality. This sentence talks about how the Civil War is testing whether or not a nation that was created to ensure liberty and equality can really survive.

9. A: This paragraph establishes that the U.S. Coast Guard is being discussed in an informational context. The other paragraphs provide supporting details.

10. A good sentence would be "Enforcement of laws and protection of the environment are just two of the many responsibilities that a member of the Coast Guard (or "Coastie") can expect to have in the line of duty." Sentence 10 basically provides a laundry list of things that Coast Guard members do on a daily basis.

11. A: Paragraph 3 gives information about what the Coast Guard does in an average day, but there is no indication as to where this very specific information comes from. Adding a line saying that the information came from the official Coast Guard Web site would add credibility.

12. C: This answer choice best sums up the information in this essay, and rounds out the writer's discussion about the organization as a whole. Answers A and B talk about the Coast Guard as a career, which isn't a theme in this essay. Answer D contradicts the information and ideas in the essay.

13. B: This source is the most reliable, and will provide the most relevant information. The other sources are either too broad or unrelated to the assigned topic.

14. A: The paragraph clearly shows the negative emotions that Brett was feeling during his mother's pregnancy. He wasn't indifferent about the situation, and he was not experiencing positive feelings about the pregnancy at this point. Answer A is the best choice.

15. Part A: A: Sentence 18 talks about how his fears are about to come true, so it gives the best description of how he is feeling.

Part B: C: Sentence 20 says: I was scared, though. In the context of this paragraph, this statement doesn't need to be made; it is implied. However, to understand the rest of what is being said, all of the other sentences are necessary.

16. D: The essay simply states that the birth of his sister was Brett's most memorable experience. It doesn't state why he feels this way.

17. A: Answer A connects back to the opening sentence in the essay and touches on the main theme of love, making it an appropriate way to conclude this writer's thoughts. The other answer choices don't really make sense in the context of what is being discussed in the final paragraph, or they do not convey the overall message of the essay.

18. Part A: D: This is the only fact. All of the other answer choices are opinions.

Part B: There are many sentences that are opinions. These are two examples.

1.No matter how long it may take us to overcome this premeditated invasion, the American people in their righteous might will win through to absolute victory.

2. But always will our whole nation remember the character of the onslaught against us.

19. A: A history textbook would provide a more inclusive description of what was going on at the time of this speech, as well as specific details about the attack on Pearl Harbor.

20. C: Roosevelt makes a strong case for the declaration of war. He draws upon facts, and develops his argument in such a way that it communicates urgency without being irrational. Solid evidence and reasoning support his claim.

21. A: The gravestones in the background, the memorial plaque listing names under the words "attack on" in the foreground, the sad boy, and the American flags make answer A the most likely choice. The boy is not standing in front of a grave. There is no indication that there is any happiness associated with this event. But, there are enough clues in the picture to infer what is going on in the scene.

22. B: There is little about this scene that is happy or joyful, which makes answers A and C inappropriate. Though there is a seriousness to the scene, there is no indication that anyone is being reprimanded, or that there is any kind of extreme negative emotion here. The overall mood of this scene is reserved and respectful, which makes B the best choice.

23. C: There isn't really any indication that any sort of statement is being made with this picture. It is also not presenting information, as much of what is in the photo needs to be interpreted. Answer C is the best choice.

24. Part A: C: The subject of the sentence should be "Ben," but the noun that follows the comma at the end of the opening phrase names the subject as "the college Ben chose." This doesn't make sense, and is an example of a misplaced or dangling modifier. The subject, "the college Ben chose," agrees with the verb "was." "Harvard" is a noun, not a preposition.

Part B: The sentence should read: Aware that his decision would affect the rest of his life, Ben chose Harvard.

25. C: An adverb is a word that modifies or describes a verb, an adjective, or another adverb. "Present" is a noun. "Wrapped" is a verb. "Professional" is a noun. "Expertly" is an adverb, and it modifies the verb "wrapped."

26. B: "Pervade" means to spread throughout or to be found throughout something. The sentence tells the reader that the excitement did something in the classroom. Answer B is the only one that makes sense.

27. A: "Fold" can be used to refer to a group, specifically a group of sheep, but also a group in general. When someone "enters the fold," they are literally or figuratively going along with a group.

28. C: Hyperventilation describes an excess of air. Hyperthermia describes an excess of heat.

29. B: The colon in this sentence correctly introduces a list of items. In answer A, the semicolon should be a comma. In answer C, there should be a question mark instead of a period. In answer D, the comma should be a semicolon.

30. A: Answer B should be "acclimate." Answer C should be "wizen." Answer D should be "allude."

31. B: Dictionaries and glossaries provide definitions of words. Indexes tell you the page of a book or other work on which a topic is mentioned. A thesaurus is a reference for synonyms and antonyms.

32. D: Paragraph 1 states that Aberystwyth is located on the West Coast of Wales.

33. C: The essay provides information on various aspects of the town of Aberystwyth, providing a portrait of the town as a whole.

34. A: Situated means to be placed in a certain location.

35. B: In an essay that is factual, proclaiming that the scenery is "gorgeous" or that a town is a "hidden luxury" is an opinion.

36. B: Paragraph 3 states that two main languages are traditionally spoken in Aberystwyth.

37. C: Paragraph 1 states, "A market town refers to European areas that have the right to have markets, which differentiates it from a city or village."

38. D: Paragraph 2 states, "Constitution Hill is a hill on the north end of Aberystwyth, which provides excellent views of Cardigan Bay and which is supported by the Aberystwyth Electric Cliff Railway."

39. B: Accessories decreased by 14%, a higher decrease than any of the other departments.

40. D: Overall sales were lowest in every department in the 4th Quarter 2008.

How to Overcome Test Anxiety

Just the thought of taking a test is enough to make most people a little nervous. A test is an important event that can have a long-term impact on your future, so it's important to take it seriously and it's natural to feel anxious about performing well. But just because anxiety is normal, that doesn't mean that it's helpful in test taking, or that you should simply accept it as part of your life. Anxiety can have a variety of effects. These effects can be mild, like making you feel slightly nervous, or severe, like blocking your ability to focus or remember even a simple detail.

If you experience test anxiety—whether severe or mild—it's important to know how to beat it. To discover this, first you need to understand what causes test anxiety.

Causes of Test Anxiety

While we often think of anxiety as an uncontrollable emotional state, it can actually be caused by simple, practical things. One of the most common causes of test anxiety is that a person does not feel adequately prepared for their test. This feeling can be the result of many different issues such as poor study habits or lack of organization, but the most common culprit is time management. Starting to study too late, failing to organize your study time to cover all of the material, or being distracted while you study will mean that you're not well prepared for the test. This may lead to cramming the night before, which will cause you to be physically and mentally exhausted for the test. Poor time management also contributes to feelings of stress, fear, and hopelessness as you realize you are not well prepared but don't know what to do about it.

Other times, test anxiety is not related to your preparation for the test but comes from unresolved fear. This may be a past failure on a test, or poor performance on tests in general. It may come from comparing yourself to others who seem to be performing better or from the stress of living up to expectations. Anxiety may be driven by fears of the future—how failure on this test would affect your educational and career goals. These fears are often completely irrational, but they can still negatively impact your test performance.

Elements of Test Anxiety

As mentioned earlier, test anxiety is considered to be an emotional state, but it has physical and mental components as well. Sometimes you may not even realize that you are suffering from test anxiety until you notice the physical symptoms. These can include trembling hands, rapid heartbeat, sweating, nausea, and tense muscles. Extreme anxiety may lead to fainting or vomiting. Obviously, any of these symptoms can have a negative impact on testing. It is important to recognize them as soon as they begin to occur so that you can address the problem before it damages your performance.

The mental components of test anxiety include trouble focusing and inability to remember learned information. During a test, your mind is on high alert, which can help you recall information and stay focused for an extended period of time. However, anxiety interferes with your mind's natural processes, causing you to blank out, even on the questions you know well. The strain of testing during anxiety makes it difficult to stay focused, especially on a test that may take several hours. Extreme anxiety can take a huge mental toll, making it difficult not only to recall test information but even to understand the test questions or pull your thoughts together.

Effects of Test Anxiety

Test anxiety is like a disease—if left untreated, it will get progressively worse. Anxiety leads to poor performance, and this reinforces the feelings of fear and failure, which in turn lead to poor performances on subsequent tests. It can grow from a mild nervousness to a crippling condition. If allowed to progress, test anxiety can have a big impact on your schooling, and consequently on your future.

Test anxiety can spread to other parts of your life. Anxiety on tests can become anxiety in any stressful situation, and blanking on a test can turn into panicking in a job situation. But fortunately, you don't have to let anxiety rule your testing and determine your grades. There are a number of relatively simple steps you can take to move past anxiety and function normally on a test and in the rest of life.

Physical Steps for Beating Test Anxiety

While test anxiety is a serious problem, the good news is that it can be overcome. It doesn't have to control your ability to think and remember information. While it may take time, you can begin taking steps today to beat anxiety.

Just as your first hint that you may be struggling with anxiety comes from the physical symptoms, the first step to treating it is also physical. Rest is crucial for having a clear, strong mind. If you are tired, it is much easier to give in to anxiety. But if you establish good sleep habits, your body and mind will be ready to perform optimally, without the strain of exhaustion. Additionally, sleeping well helps you to retain information better, so you're more likely to recall the answers when you see the test questions.

Getting good sleep means more than going to bed on time. It's important to allow your brain time to relax. Take study breaks from time to time so it doesn't get overworked, and don't study right before bed. Take time to rest your mind before trying to rest your body, or you may find it difficult to fall asleep.

Along with sleep, other aspects of physical health are important in preparing for a test. Good nutrition is vital for good brain function. Sugary foods and drinks may give a burst of energy but this burst is followed by a crash, both physically and emotionally. Instead, fuel your body with protein and vitamin-rich foods.

Also, drink plenty of water. Dehydration can lead to headaches and exhaustion, especially if your brain is already under stress from the rigors of the test. Particularly if your test is a long one, drink water during the breaks. And if possible, take an energy-boosting snack to eat between sections.

Along with sleep and diet, a third important part of physical health is exercise. Maintaining a steady workout schedule is helpful, but even taking 5-minute study breaks to walk can help get your blood pumping faster and clear your head. Exercise also releases endorphins, which contribute to a positive feeling and can help combat test anxiety.

When you nurture your physical health, you are also contributing to your mental health. If your body is healthy, your mind is much more likely to be healthy as well. So take time to rest, nourish your body with healthy food and water, and get moving as much as possible. Taking these physical steps will make you stronger and more able to take the mental steps necessary to overcome test anxiety.

Mental Steps for Beating Test Anxiety

Working on the mental side of test anxiety can be more challenging, but as with the physical side, there are clear steps you can take to overcome it. As mentioned earlier, test anxiety often stems from lack of preparation, so the obvious solution is to prepare for the test. Effective studying may be the most important weapon you have for beating test anxiety, but you can and should employ several other mental tools to combat fear.

First, boost your confidence by reminding yourself of past success—tests or projects that you aced. If you're putting as much effort into preparing for this test as you did for those, there's no reason you should expect to fail here. Work hard to prepare; then trust your preparation.

Second, surround yourself with encouraging people. It can be helpful to find a study group, but be sure that the people you're around will encourage a positive attitude. If you spend time with others who are anxious or cynical, this will only contribute to your own anxiety. Look for others who are motivated to study hard from a desire to succeed, not from a fear of failure.

Third, reward yourself. A test is physically and mentally tiring, even without anxiety, and it can be helpful to have something to look forward to. Plan an activity following the test, regardless of the outcome, such as going to a movie or getting ice cream.

When you are taking the test, if you find yourself beginning to feel anxious, remind yourself that you know the material. Visualize successfully completing the test. Then take a few deep, relaxing breaths and return to it. Work through the questions carefully but with confidence, knowing that you are capable of succeeding.

Developing a healthy mental approach to test taking will also aid in other areas of life. Test anxiety affects more than just the actual test—it can be damaging to your mental health and even contribute to depression. It's important to beat test anxiety before it becomes a problem for more than testing.

Study Strategy

Being prepared for the test is necessary to combat anxiety, but what does being prepared look like? You may study for hours on end and still not feel prepared. What you need is a strategy for test prep. The next few pages outline our recommended steps to help you plan out and conquer the challenge of preparation.

Step 1: Scope Out the Test

Learn everything you can about the format (multiple choice, essay, etc.) and what will be on the test. Gather any study materials, course outlines, or sample exams that may be available. Not only will this help you to prepare, but knowing what to expect can help to alleviate test anxiety.

Step 2: Map Out the Material

Look through the textbook or study guide and make note of how many chapters or sections it has. Then divide these over the time you have. For example, if a book has 15 chapters and you have five days to study, you need to cover three chapters each day. Even better, if you have the time, leave an extra day at the end for overall review after you have gone through the material in depth.

If time is limited, you may need to prioritize the material. Look through it and make note of which sections you think you already have a good grasp on, and which need review. While you are studying, skim quickly through the familiar sections and take more time on the challenging parts.

Write out your plan so you don't get lost as you go. Having a written plan also helps you feel more in control of the study, so anxiety is less likely to arise from feeling overwhelmed at the amount to cover.

STEP 3: GATHER YOUR TOOLS

Decide what study method works best for you. Do you prefer to highlight in the book as you study and then go back over the highlighted portions? Or do you type out notes of the important information? Or is it helpful to make flashcards that you can carry with you? Assemble the pens, index cards, highlighters, post-it notes, and any other materials you may need so you won't be distracted by getting up to find things while you study.

If you're having a hard time retaining the information or organizing your notes, experiment with different methods. For example, try color-coding by subject with colored pens, highlighters, or post-it notes. If you learn better by hearing, try recording yourself reading your notes so you can listen while in the car, working out, or simply sitting at your desk. Ask a friend to quiz you from your flashcards, or try teaching someone the material to solidify it in your mind.

STEP 4: CREATE YOUR ENVIRONMENT

It's important to avoid distractions while you study. This includes both the obvious distractions like visitors and the subtle distractions like an uncomfortable chair (or a too-comfortable couch that makes you want to fall asleep). Set up the best study environment possible: good lighting and a comfortable work area. If background music helps you focus, you may want to turn it on, but otherwise keep the room quiet. If you are using a computer to take notes, be sure you don't have any other windows open, especially applications like social media, games, or anything else that could distract you. Silence your phone and turn off notifications. Be sure to keep water close by so you stay hydrated while you study (but avoid unhealthy drinks and snacks).

Also, take into account the best time of day to study. Are you freshest first thing in the morning? Try to set aside some time then to work through the material. Is your mind clearer in the afternoon or evening? Schedule your study session then. Another method is to study at the same time of day that you will take the test, so that your brain gets used to working on the material at that time and will be ready to focus at test time.

STEP 5: STUDY!

Once you have done all the study preparation, it's time to settle into the actual studying. Sit down, take a few moments to settle your mind so you can focus, and begin to follow your study plan. Don't give in to distractions or let yourself procrastinate. This is your time to prepare so you'll be ready to fearlessly approach the test. Make the most of the time and stay focused.

Of course, you don't want to burn out. If you study too long you may find that you're not retaining the information very well. Take regular study breaks. For example, taking five minutes out of every hour to walk briskly, breathing deeply and swinging your arms, can help your mind stay fresh.

As you get to the end of each chapter or section, it's a good idea to do a quick review. Remind yourself of what you learned and work on any difficult parts. When you feel that you've mastered the material, move on to the next part. At the end of your study session, briefly skim through your notes again.

But while review is helpful, cramming last minute is NOT. If at all possible, work ahead so that you won't need to fit all your study into the last day. Cramming overloads your brain with more information than it can process and retain, and your tired mind may struggle to recall even previously learned information when it is overwhelmed with last-minute study. Also, the urgent nature of cramming and the stress placed on your brain contribute to anxiety. You'll be more likely to go to the test feeling unprepared and having trouble thinking clearly.

So don't cram, and don't stay up late before the test, even just to review your notes at a leisurely pace. Your brain needs rest more than it needs to go over the information again. In fact, plan to finish your studies by noon or early afternoon the day before the test. Give your brain the rest of the day to relax or focus on other things, and get a good night's sleep. Then you will be fresh for the test and better able to recall what you've studied.

Step 6: Take a Practice Test

Many courses offer sample tests, either online or in the study materials. This is an excellent resource to check whether you have mastered the material, as well as to prepare for the test format and environment.

Check the test format ahead of time: the number of questions, the type (multiple choice, free response, etc.), and the time limit. Then create a plan for working through them. For example, if you have 30 minutes to take a 60-question test, your limit is 30 seconds per question. Spend less time on the questions you know well so that you can take more time on the difficult ones.

If you have time to take several practice tests, take the first one open book, with no time limit. Work through the questions at your own pace and make sure you fully understand them. Gradually work up to taking a test under test conditions: sit at a desk with all study materials put away and set a timer. Pace yourself to make sure you finish the test with time to spare and go back to check your answers if you have time.

After each test, check your answers. On the questions you missed, be sure you understand why you missed them. Did you misread the question (tests can use tricky wording)? Did you forget the information? Or was it something you hadn't learned? Go back and study any shaky areas that the practice tests reveal.

Taking these tests not only helps with your grade, but also aids in combating test anxiety. If you're already used to the test conditions, you're less likely to worry about it, and working through tests until you're scoring well gives you a confidence boost. Go through the practice tests until you feel comfortable, and then you can go into the test knowing that you're ready for it.

Test Tips

On test day, you should be confident, knowing that you've prepared well and are ready to answer the questions. But aside from preparation, there are several test day strategies you can employ to maximize your performance.

First, as stated before, get a good night's sleep the night before the test (and for several nights before that, if possible). Go into the test with a fresh, alert mind rather than staying up late to study.

Try not to change too much about your normal routine on the day of the test. It's important to eat a nutritious breakfast, but if you normally don't eat breakfast at all, consider eating just a protein bar. If you're a coffee drinker, go ahead and have your normal coffee. Just make sure you time it so that the caffeine doesn't wear off right in the middle of your test. Avoid sugary beverages, and drink enough water to stay hydrated but not so much that you need a restroom break 10 minutes into the test. If your test isn't first thing in the morning, consider going for a walk or doing a light workout before the test to get your blood flowing.

Allow yourself enough time to get ready, and leave for the test with plenty of time to spare so you won't have the anxiety of scrambling to arrive in time. Another reason to be early is to select a good seat. It's helpful to sit away from doors and windows, which can be distracting. Find a good seat, get out your supplies, and settle your mind before the test begins.

When the test begins, start by going over the instructions carefully, even if you already know what to expect. Make sure you avoid any careless mistakes by following the directions.

Then begin working through the questions, pacing yourself as you've practiced. If you're not sure on an answer, don't spend too much time on it, and don't let it shake your confidence. Either skip it and come back later, or eliminate as many wrong answers as possible and guess among the remaining ones. Don't dwell on these questions as you continue—put them out of your mind and focus on what lies ahead.

Be sure to read all of the answer choices, even if you're sure the first one is the right answer. Sometimes you'll find a better one if you keep reading. But don't second-guess yourself if you do immediately know the answer. Your gut instinct is usually right. Don't let test anxiety rob you of the information you know.

If you have time at the end of the test (and if the test format allows), go back and review your answers. Be cautious about changing any, since your first instinct tends to be correct, but make sure you didn't misread any of the questions or accidentally mark the wrong answer choice. Look over any you skipped and make an educated guess.

At the end, leave the test feeling confident. You've done your best, so don't waste time worrying about your performance or wishing you could change anything. Instead, celebrate the successful completion of this test. And finally, use this test to learn how to deal with anxiety even better next time.

Review Video: Test Anxiety
Visit mometrix.com/academy and enter code: 100340

Important Qualification

Not all anxiety is created equal. If your test anxiety is causing major issues in your life beyond the classroom or testing center, or if you are experiencing troubling physical symptoms related to your anxiety, it may be a sign of a serious physiological or psychological condition. If this sounds like your situation, we strongly encourage you to seek professional help.

Thank You

We at Mometrix would like to extend our heartfelt thanks to you, our friend and patron, for allowing us to play a part in your journey. It is a privilege to serve people from all walks of life who are unified in their commitment to building the best future they can for themselves.

The preparation you devote to these important testing milestones may be the most valuable educational opportunity you have for making a real difference in your life. We encourage you to put your heart into it—that feeling of succeeding, overcoming, and yes, conquering will be well worth the hours you've invested.

We want to hear your story, your struggles and your successes, and if you see any opportunities for us to improve our materials so we can help others even more effectively in the future, please share that with us as well. **The team at Mometrix would be absolutely thrilled to hear from you!** So please, send us an email (support@mometrix.com) and let's stay in touch.

If you'd like some additional help, check out these other resources we offer for your exam:
http://MometrixFlashcards.com/CCSS

Online Resources

Due to our efforts to try to keep this book to a manageable length, we've created a link that will give you access to all of your online resources:

mometrix.com/resources719/ccg7ela

It's Your Moment, Let's Celebrate It!

Share your story @mometrixtestpreparation